Turkey

Turkey

BY TAMRA B. ORR

Enchantment of the World™
Second Series

CHILDREN'S PRESS®

An Imprint of Scholastic Inc.

New York   Toronto   London   Auckland   Sydney
Mexico City   New Delhi   Hong Kong
Danbury, Connecticut

Frontispiece: **Green Tomb, Bursa**

Consultant: Christine M. Philliou, PhD, Associate Professor of History, Columbia University, New York, New York
Please note: All statistics are as up-to-date as possible at the time of publication.

Book production by The Design Lab

Library of Congress Cataloging-in-Publication Data
Orr, Tamra.
 Turkey / by Tamra B. Orr.
  pages cm. — (Enchantment of the world)
 Includes bibliographical references and index.
 ISBN 978-0-531-20792-5 (library binding)
 1. Turkey—Juvenile literature. 2. Turkey—History—Juvenile literature. 3. Turkey—Civilization—Juvenile literature. 4. Turkey—Geography. 5. Turkey—Politics and government—Juvenile literature. I. Title.
 DR417.4.O77 2015
 956.1—dc23   2014001868

1 2 3 4 5 6 7 8 9 10 R 24 23 22 21 20 19 18 17 16 15

Carpet merchant

Contents

Left to right: **Family, Republic Day, playing soccer, shepherd, voter**

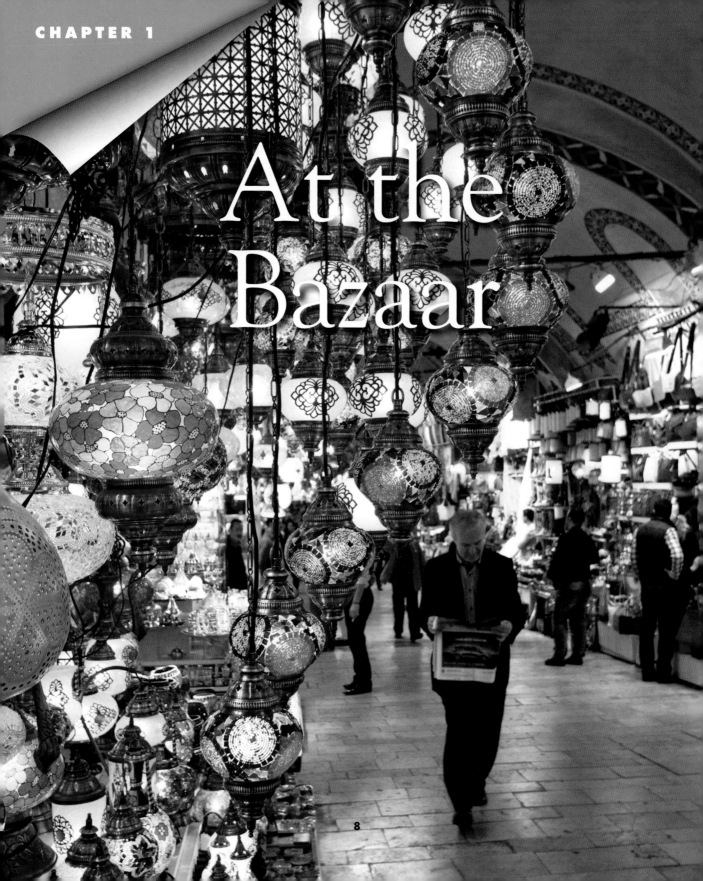

CHAPTER 1

At the Bazaar

POP QUIZ! IS THE NATION OF TURKEY IN EUROPE OR IN Asia? The answer is both! Turkey stretches across the boundary between southeastern Europe and southwestern Asia, and its largest city, Istanbul, has a foot on both continents. Where is a good place to get a crash course in Turkey's history, culture, people, and language? Try the *Kapalicarsi*, or Grand Bazaar, in Istanbul.

The Grand Bazaar certainly earns its name! It covers more than sixty streets, has twenty-two gates, and contains more than five thousand shops. It also includes multiple fountains and wells, two mosques, and many restaurants, cafés, and teahouses. It even has its own post office, police station, and fire station.

Opposite: **Glass lamps brighten the halls at the Grand Bazaar.**

The Grand Bazaar is one of the largest covered markets in the world. It is also the oldest, since it was first built in the fifteenth century on the order of the Ottoman ruler Sultan Mehmed the Conqueror. Each night, one hundred soldiers guarded the bazaar. The market was rebuilt at the end of the nineteenth century after a destructive earthquake hit the city.

Walking into the market is like walking into a wall of smells, sounds, and sights. Walking down its streets you are struck one moment by the smell of smoky incense and the next by the sharp odor of spices like mint, cumin, and oregano. The aroma of fragrant oils wafts by on a breeze, followed by a whiff of gentle herbs.

Approximately four hundred thousand visitors stroll through the streets of the market every day. Inside, more than twenty thousand employees go to work, so the bazaar is always

In 1453, the Ottoman leader Mehmed the Conqueror (on horseback) gained control of Istanbul, known at the time as Constantinople. He made the city the capital of the Ottoman Empire.

Shops at the Grand Bazaar display small mountains of brightly colored spices and tea powders.

alive with the buzz of voices. Many languages are spoken here, and salespeople in shops will easily flow from one language to the next to try to lure in as many customers as possible.

As powerful as the noise is, it pales in comparison with the sights! Rows of silver and gold jewelry sparkle like stars under the dim lights. Lines of fresh fruit and vegetables look like rainbows. Turkey is the biggest producer of hazelnuts in the world, and here visitors can find them shelled, peeled, salted, plain, roasted, or ground. Nearby are heaps of dried figs, apricots, and raisins.

Hand-painted plates and bowls in bright patterns are stacked on shelves, covered in patterns that have been handed down for generations. Piles of handmade silk rugs fill carpet shops. Some of the most exquisite carpets can take from six months to four years to complete. Millions of knots go into every pattern.

People from all over the world walk through the aisles and employees call out, doing all they can to catch the eye of possible customers. If you stop to look, be prepared to be shown around the entire store. Many businesses offer visitors a cup of apple tea as they look around.

Many goods in the market don't have a price tag. The merchants in the market expect their customers to haggle. This means the buyer and seller negotiate and settle on a price.

Merchants relax with cups of tea. Turks drink tea in clear glass cups.

To end up with a good price, the buyer should at first show almost no interest in any of the products. Finally, the buyer asks about a price. Whatever amount the salesperson says, it is not the real amount. It is much higher than what the seller will actually accept. Customers are expected to protest, and offer less. Then the back and forth process of haggling begins. If the salesperson says a necklace is $50, the customer might offer $20. Then back and for they go until they settle on $35, a price that pleases them both.

A rug merchant points out details of a carpet to customers. Different regions in Turkey have traditionally produced carpets in different styles.

Young Turks relax at a café in the Beyoglu neighborhood of Istanbul. This lively neighborhood is filled with restaurants and shops.

After spending a day at the bazaar, visitors have a better idea of what Turkey is all about. They've heard the language and seen the history reflected in age-old patterns and crafts. They've experienced the culture in the tea and the hospitality, and they've tasted the food that blends Asian, European, and African influences. But there's a lot more to learn about Turkey. It is a fascinating country, full of ancient artifacts and modern businesses, soaring mountains and busy coastlines. It invites people from all over the world to explore and enjoy it!

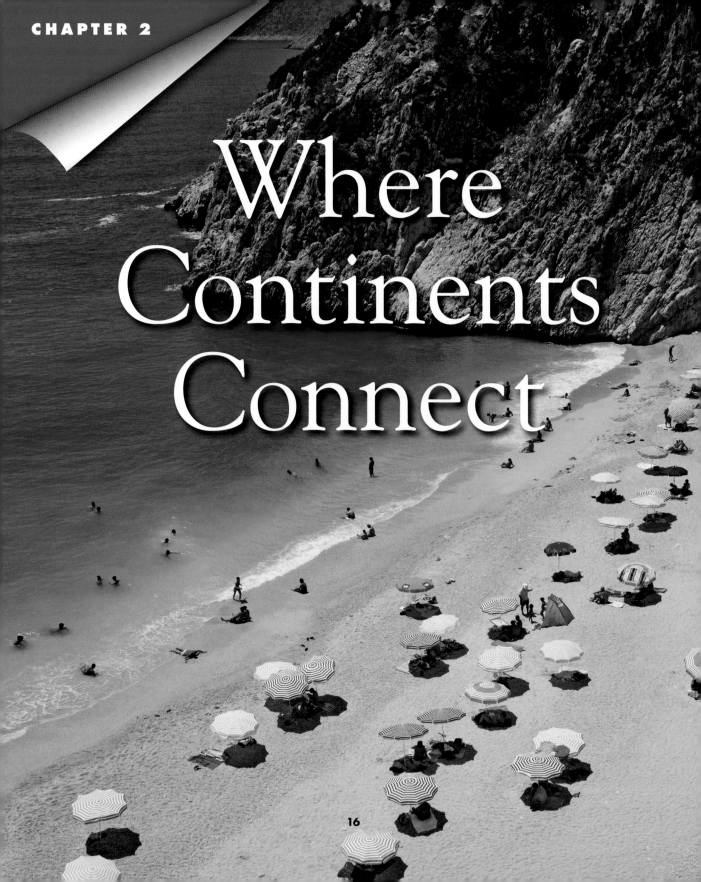

CHAPTER 2

Where Continents Connect

WELCOME TO TURKEY, A NATION SPLIT BETWEEN two continents. Thrace is the name of the portion found in Europe. It is quite small, only about 3 percent of the entire country. Anatolia, the name of the Asian portion, is slightly larger than the states of Texas and Louisiana put together.

The Sea of Marmara and the Bosporus Strait separate the European and Asian parts of Turkey. These two bodies of water connect the Black Sea, which lies to the north of Turkey, and the Aegean Sea, an arm of the Mediterranean that lies to the west. The main part of the Mediterranean lies to the south of Turkey. Altogether, the country has about 4,500 miles (7,200 kilometers) of coastline, which ranges from popular tourist beaches to wild areas that few people ever see. Turkey also borders eight countries: Greece, Bulgaria, Georgia, Armenia, Azerbaijan, Iran, Iraq, and Syria.

Opposite: **Turkey's Mediterranean coast is a mix of steep cliffs and beautiful beaches.**

The Busy Bosporus

Separating Europe and Asia and linking the Black Sea to the Sea of Marmara is a 19-mile (30 km) strait called the Bosporus. Boats on the Bosporus travel past buildings representing a wealth of Turkish history. They pass six-hundred-year old fortresses, magnificent Ottoman palaces, and current cultural sites such as the Istanbul Museum of Modern Art.

The Bosporus is like a water highway, ranging in width from 0.5 miles to 2.3 miles (0.8 to 3.7 km) and in depth from 120 feet to 408 feet (37 to 124 m). Every day, boats travel up and down the water like a system of city buses. Tens of thousands of vessels travel these waters every year, including containerships, Russian submarines, oil and gas tankers, naval vessels, passenger ferries, fishing boats, and luxury speedboats. Just like on the road, traffic jams and accidents are common. To help with this problem, Turkish prime minister

Recep Erdogan wants to spend $10 billion building a 31-mile-long (50 km) canal on the European side of Turkey. Working ships would use the new canal, and the Bosporus would be for pleasure boats and tourists only.

The Many Turkeys

Turkey is divided into seven regions. These regions have vastly different land and climates.

The Aegean is in the western part of Turkey. It takes up about 11 percent of the land and is renowned for its blue waters, green hills, and white beaches. Fishing harbors dot the coastline. The land is wet, green, and fertile, allowing olive groves and pine trees to thrive. The ancient Greek ruins of Troy, Pergamum, and Ephesus are found in the Aegean region.

The northwestern area of Turkey, where Europe and Asia connect, is called the Marmara region. It covers approximately 9 percent of the country. Although much of this

Turkey's Geographic Features

Area: 302,535 square miles (783,562 sq km)

Highest Elevation: Mount Ararat 16,949 feet (5,166 m)

Lowest Elevation: Sea level, along the coasts

Length of Coastline: 4,500 miles (7,200 km)

Longest River: Kizil, 734 miles (1,182 km)

Largest Lake: Lake Van, 1,450 square miles (3,755 sq km)

Hottest Region: Southeast Anatolia, average high temperature of 95°F (35°C) in July

Coldest Region: Eastern Anatolia, average low temperature of 5°F (–15°C) in January

Wettest Region: Eastern Black Sea coastal region, 96 inches (244 cm) per year

Driest Region: Southeast Anatolia 14 inches (35 cm) per year

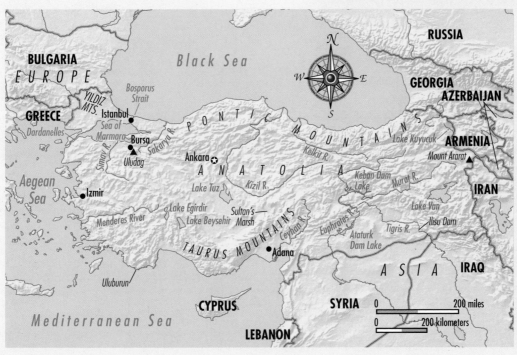

region is lowlands, it also includes Mount Uludag and the Yildiz Mountains, as well as a number of islands in the Aegean Sea and Sea of Marmara. The busy city of Istanbul is in this region, along with Bursa, a city surrounded by forests and sweeping meadows.

The Mediterranean region lies in the south of the country, along the Mediterranean Sea. Although it frequently suffers droughts and floods, it is a productive agricultural region. Crops grown in the Mediterranean region include grapes, bananas, rice, cotton, and citrus fruits such as oranges and mandarins. This region, which covers 15 percent of the

Some of the craggy peaks in the Taurus Mountains top 10,000 feet (3,000 m).

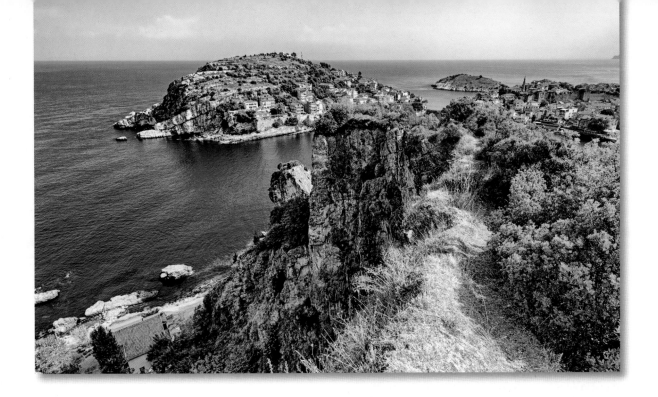

country, includes some of the nation's biggest cities, including Adana and Antalya. The Taurus Mountains crowd the coast, separating the Mediterranean region from central Anatolia. Part of this mountain range features a stunning karst landscape. Karst occurs when underground rivers dissolve limestone rock, leaving behind craggy gray rocks riddled with holes, cracks, and caves.

The Black Sea region is a long, narrow strip along the north side of the country, covering about 18 percent of the nation's land area. It includes a rocky coastline, deep valleys, and long deltas fed by river waters. The Pontic Mountains rise to heights of nearly 13,000 feet (4,000 meters) near the coast of the Black Sea. This region is rich in plant life—more than seven thousand species of plants grow here. The region's heavy rainfall helps produce abundant crops of hazelnuts and tea.

The port town of Amasra lies on the Black Sea. The sea's name does not come from the water's color. Rather, it comes from the fact that sailors considered the Black Sea dangerous because of its sudden, violent storms.

Looking at Turkey's Cities

The largest city in Turkey is not its capital, Ankara, but the city of Istanbul. With a population of 13.7 million, this city is overflowing with history and culture. Over the centuries, the city has had three different names. Originally called Byzantium, it became Constantinople in the fourth century CE when it came under the control of Constantine I, and then Istanbul under the Ottoman Empire. The city is a mix of ancient and modern. It is full of majestic sites, including the vast Blue Mosque (right), famed for its beautiful blue tiles, and the Hagia Sophia, a former church that is now a museum. Shoppers fill traditional markets such as the Grand Bazaar and the Spice Market and modern shopping malls. Istanbul is also the center of Turkish culture, finance, and media.

Ankara is the nation's second-largest city, with a population of 4.6 million, followed by Izmir with 3.4 million people. Izmir, which lies on the Aegean coast, is the site of ancient settlements dating back at least five thousand years, and the Greek city of Smyrna was established there more than three thousand years ago. By the 1600s, it became a thriving port city with a diverse population. Although many of its historic buildings have been destroyed in fires and earthquakes, some of the ruins of ancient Smyrna remain. Today, Izmir is a thriving industrial city, a major producer of goods such as food products, textiles, and chemicals.

Bursa, the fourth-largest city in Turkey, has about 2 million people. The city, located in northwestern Anatolia, was once the center of Turkey's silk and spice trade. Today, it remains an important industrial city, excelling in automobile and textile manufacturing. The city boasts many fine examples of Ottoman architecture (left), which features arched portals, tiled spires, detailed decorations, and houses with square bay windows. One of the most notable buildings is the Grand Mosque, which was built in about 1400 and features twenty domes.

Central Anatolia takes up about a fifth of Turkey's landmass, making it the country's second-largest region. Lying between two mountain ranges, this region is sometimes known as Turkey's heartland. Wooded areas cover the north, but the rest of the land consists mostly of wide, flat plateaus. Much of this territory is used to graze animals. Some crops are grown in this area, but limited rainfall and extreme cold and heat can make farming difficult. Central Anatolia is home to modern industrial cities such as Ankara and Konya, but it is also an area rich in history and has seen many civilizations come and go. Glimpses into the country's past are seen in Cappadocia, a dry region of soft volcanic rock that has eroded into towers and cones. Early Christians carved

The slender, eroded formations in Cappadocia are known as fairy chimneys.

out churches and homes in the soft rock. Some people even created entire underground cities. Until a few decades ago, "cave homes" were common in the region.

The largest region in Turkey is eastern Anatolia. Although it covers 21 percent of the country, it has the smallest population, in large part because of its cold climate and rugged, barren landscape. Eastern Anatolia features many high mountain peaks, including Mount Ararat, the nation's highest peak, and several extinct volcanoes. It is also home to Turkey's largest lake, Lake Van, which stretches across about 1,450 square miles (3,755 square kilometers) near the border with Iran.

Southeastern Anatolia is the smallest of Turkey's seven regions, covering less than 10 percent of the country. It covers the area along the Tigris and Euphrates Rivers. In the past,

The Resting Place of Noah's Ark?

If you've heard the story of Noah's Ark, chances are you've heard of Mount Ararat. Located in the easternmost part of Anatolia, this huge mountain is actually a dormant volcano. It has two peaks about seven miles (11 km) apart. The highest peak, Great Ararat, is the country's highest point at 16,949 feet (5,166 m). The second peak, Little Ararat, rises to 12,782 feet (3,896 m).

Covered in snow, this mountain attracts hikers and climbers from all over the world. Some climb to the top just for the excitement and the challenge. Others have climbed in hopes of finding evidence that Noah's Ark did in fact exist and come to a final resting place atop the mountain. To date, no evidence has ever been found.

The Dam Issue

What happens when the government wants to make a change—and the people object? That is the very issue going on in Turkey today with the construction of the Ilisu Dam located on the southeastern Tigris River. While many government officials are sure that building the dam will help generate needed power, other people think the dam is a huge mistake.

Leaders in Turkey explain that the dam will create environmentally clean electricity, as well as help irrigate dry areas so that they can become fertile farmland. Construction of the dam creates jobs, and after its completion the area will attract visitors and tourists, especially those who enjoy water sports.

While using the power of the many rivers found in Turkey sounds like a good idea, many people in Turkey, including historians and environmentalists, are objecting. The construction of this dam will submerge 121 square miles (313 sq km) of land underwater, including the historic town of Hasankeyf (below). As many as sev-

enty thousand people will be forced out of their homes and into other cities. In addition, hundreds of important sites, from ancient cave dwellings to medieval royal tombs (above), will become sunken treasure, covered by water. A number of animal species, including the striped hyena and the Euphrates soft-shelled turtle, will also be threatened as their habitats are destroyed.

In 2008, Turkey promised to move some of the archaeological treasures to a nearby cultural park in order to preserve them, but that did not solve the problem. These ancient structures cannot be easily taken apart, moved, and put back together. Ercan Ayboga, a spokesperson for a group protesting the dam, says attempting to move these treasures is a mistake. "It is totally impractical and technically impossible," he says.

Construction on the dam continued, and Turkey hopes to have it completed sometime in 2014. The Turkish government strongly believes that the dam will make life better for everyone in Turkey. "Our country needs energy, and we are trying to meet that need," said Mahmut Dundar, general manager of the project. "This jumbo project is of the utmost strategic and economic importance to our country."

people have sometimes struggled to grow crops in this dry, cold area. But in recent years, more hydroelectric dams have been built, bringing water to the region. Today, the region produces crops such as wheat, barley, and pistachios.

Weather Report

Turkey is a diverse land, ranging from soaring mountains to balmy beaches to desolate valley, so its climate is also diverse. In the Marmara area, the summers are warm and sunny, and winters are mild. The Aegean and Mediterranean regions tend to be hot and dry in the summer, and have very brief winters.

A shepherd tends to his flock in the snowy mountains of southeastern Anatolia. Snow often falls in the region from November until late April.

Quaking and Blowing

Turkey is known for many beautiful things, from intricate rugs to colorful tulips, but it is also known for something less beautiful—powerful earthquakes. One of the country's biggest earthquakes happened in 1999. Measuring 7.6 on the Richter scale, a measure of an earthquake's energy, it centered on the city of Izmit, east of Istanbul. The quake killed more than seventeen thousand people and caused billions of dollars of damage.

In October 2011, a strong earthquake hit southeastern Turkey. For 30 seconds, the earth shook. The vibration could be felt for hundreds of square miles, all the way into Armenia and Iran. Hundreds of people were killed and many others were missing. Buildings crashed to the ground, and highways collapsed. A number of aftershocks made rescue and recovery challenging.

Turkey has also suffered astonishing windstorms. In April 2012, extremely strong southwestern winds known as *lodos* swept through Istanbul. The winds, blowing up to 62 miles per hour (100 kph), injured dozens of people, collapsed roofs, sent construction scaffolding crashing down on cars below, and even set a yacht on fire. Fishing ships came to the rescue of the many people jumping into the water to escape the flames.

The Black Sea region receives the most rainfall, with some parts averaging nearly 100 inches (250 centimeters) a year. During the winter months, snow often blows through as well. Extreme heat and heavy snowfall are common in central Anatolia.

Eastern and southeastern Anatolia have some of the most extreme weather conditions. Temperatures often rise above 100 degrees Fahrenheit (38 degrees Celsius) during the summer months and can drop to −40°F (−40°C) in the winter. The mountains also experience harsh weather, especially in the winter when snow is on the ground for four months or more.

CHAPTER 3

Nature's Superpower

WHEN TURKISH BIOLOGIST CAGAN SEKERCIOGLU wrote about the incredible wildlife found in Turkey for *National Geographic* magazine, he called the country "the biodiversity superpower of Europe." It is easy to see why. Because of its varied landscape and climate, the country is rich in all types of life. One-third of the nine thousand plant species found inside the country's borders are endemic, meaning they grow only in that country. Many species of reptiles, amphibians, birds, and fish are also endemic.

From the Ground

About 15 percent of Turkey is covered in forest. Chestnut, sycamore, and pine trees thrive in the northwest, while the Black Sea region has mountain slopes blanketed in oaks and maples. Wild olive and licorice trees grow in the southwest.

Only in Turkey

Would you like to see a Black Sea viper slither by or a Bolland's blue butterfly flutter past? If so, you had better head to Turkey, because that is the only place these animal species can be found. Turkey is home to five unique mammal species, eleven amphibian species, thirteen reptile species, and fifty-two freshwater fish species not found in any other part of the world. In addition, about three thousand plant species grow only in Turkey, including the Turkish peony (right).

Wildflowers carpet the land in Cappadocia.

With the thousands of plant species throughout Turkey, springtime can be breathtaking, as colorful petals unfold. Lilies

Turkey's Tulips

Many people think of Holland when they think of tulips, but that is not where they are originally from. Tulips are native to Turkey, and they are its national flower. These bold, colorful flowers were not brought to Holland until the sixteenth century. The period of Turkish history from 1718 to 1730 is known as the Tulip Era. During those years, under the rule of Ahmed III, the image of tulips could be seen almost everywhere in what is now Turkey. Tulip images were included in carpets, tiles, and clothing. Tulips were planted in the royal gardens. Having rows of these bright flowers indicated wealth and status. They were so precious, in fact, that only privileged people were allowed to buy or sell them. Anyone who had tulips without permission from the sultan (king) could be exiled.

Today, Turkey still takes pride in its tulips. Every spring since 2006, Istanbul's government has planted millions of tulip bulbs throughout the city. In 2013, about 13 million tulips were planted in parks and other areas. The Istanbul Tulip Festival, held each April, draws visitors from all over the world to admire the beauty of this historic flower.

and roses are common, as are tulips, the national flower. The countryside also blossoms with red poppies, pink and white oleanders, bell-shaped snowdrops, and delicate cyclamens.

In the Air

As beautiful and colorful as Turkey's plant life is, so is its wildlife. The country is home to more than eighty thousand species of crawling, flying, swimming, and walking creatures.

Hundreds of types of birds either live in Turkey year-round or make a stop there during their migration from Africa to Asia or Europe. In the spring months, the bird population in Turkey balloons. During this time, more than a quarter of a million white storks wing across the sky. Some are just passing through, while others stay long enough to build nests at the top of church spires and telephone poles.

White storks are carnivores. They eat a wide variety of creatures, including snakes.

For the Birds

Most tourists do not know Lake Kuyucuk, but it is quite popular with birds. At least half of the bird species found year-round in Turkey, as well as many of the species migrating between eastern Europe and Africa, spend time at this lake in the Kars Province of eastern Turkey.

Until 2009, a dirt road cut across the lake. But now, thanks to many months of hard work by dedicated conservationists and local villagers, that dirt road has been transformed into a 600-foot-long (180 m) island that provides a haven for the birds. To create the island, workers moved tons of dirt and built strong island walls. Trees were planted on the island's northern side.

This new island gives birds like ruddy shelducks, sand plovers, water rails (left), and jack snipes the chance to roost and breed in peace. The birds nesting on the island are completely safe from foxes, dogs, cats, sheep—and people—all of which can be found elsewhere around the lake.

Turkey has more than seventy bird sanctuaries, where birds are protected. Every year, hundreds of thousands of ducks, egrets, flamingos, and pelicans stop in a place called Sultan's Marsh in central Anatolia. Sultan's Marsh is a wild mix of freshwater, saltwater, and mudflats. During the migration season, 250 different bird species can be found in this vital wetland.

On Land

Animals found roaming the ground in Turkey include wolves, foxes, bears, deer, and wild cats. The Kars region in northeastern Turkey is home to many large animals, including brown bears, gray wolves, and lynx. For a number of years,

The European agama lives in rocky areas in Turkey. Many agamas grow more than 1 foot (30 cm) long.

environmental researchers have been studying Kars to better understand how to protect and support the animals living there. A number of animals have been killed by hunters and in car accidents, and the habitat area keeps shrinking.

In 2010, Turkey began working to create the first wildlife corridor to protect these species. It will be 50 miles (80 km) long, and cover 58,000 acres (23,500 hectares). It will ensure that the largest animals have enough room to live and breed, without danger from humans.

Turkey is also home to more than 120 reptile species. Many kinds of snakes live in Turkey, including poisonous vipers. The country is also home to tortoises and a variety of lizards, including skinks and agamas.

In the Water

The brilliant blue waters of the Aegean Sea harbor a large number of species, including groupers, eels, octopuses, and parrot fish. Two unusual animals found in the waters of the Aegean coast are the loggerhead turtle and the monk seal. Loggerheads get their name because of their sizable heads.

Parrot fish are named for their birdlike beaks, which they use to scrape algae off of rock and coral.

A Gazelle Surprise

It seems like there is always another story in the news about some type of animal that has become—or is about to become—extinct. Thus, it was a delight in spring 2009 when researchers found the opposite. They discovered 250 mountain gazelles living in the Hatay Province of southern Turkey. This type of gazelle lives in the mountains, foothills, and coastal plains of the Arabian Peninsula, and was facing possible extinction. There are fewer than 15,000 of them left in the wild, because they have long been hunted and they have lost their habitat. Now that they have been found in Turkey, the government will work to protect the species.

They need the huge heads to support their powerful jaws, which they use to crunch and crush their hard-shelled meals of clams or sea urchins. The females, which are about 3 feet (1 m) long, pull themselves up on the beach to lay their eggs in the sand. Once laid, the eggs have to stay covered for two months before the baby turtles are ready to hatch. However, curious tourists often disturb these beach nests, harming the eggs. For the babies that do manage to hatch, the trip from beach to ocean is long and dangerous. Naturally drawn to the

Loggerheads are the most common turtle in the Mediterranean Sea. They spend much of their time feeding in the shallow coastal waters.

sparkle of reflected moonlight on the water's surface, these tiny creatures are often distracted by the sparkle of city lights instead, and crawl in the wrong—and fatal—direction.

Another animal that is in great danger in Turkey is the monk seal. Only a few hundred of these animals remain in the entire world. Construction along the coast, water pollution, tourism, and overfishing have all contributed to their decline. About fifty of these remaining monk seals live in the Mediterranean Sea between Turkey and Greece. In 1991, Turkey set up more than a dozen protected areas to help keep the monk seals safe. In these places, no diving, fishing, or boating is permitted. Since these creatures are not able to live in captivity, it is essential to make it possible for them to live and breed in their natural habitats.

A monk seal swims near the Turkish coast. Although monk seals once gathered on beaches in the Mediterranean Sea, they now seek out more isolated coastal caves, away from people.

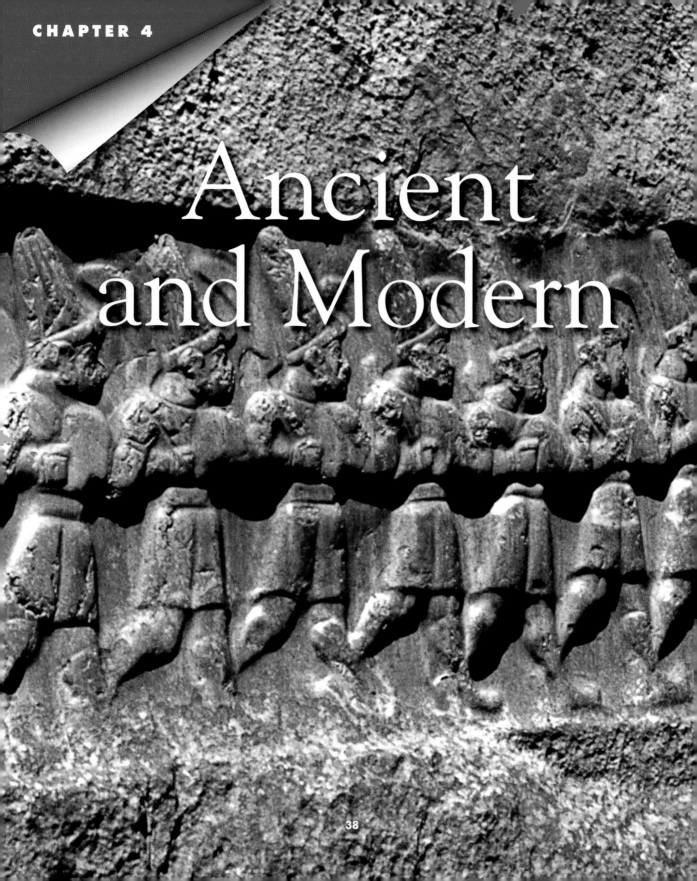

CHAPTER 4

Ancient
and Modern

CAN YOU IMAGINE BEING THE FIRST PERSON TO discover a people that had been lost to time? That is what happened when a French archaeologist named Charles Texier came to Bogazkale in central Anatolia in 1834. While he was there, he spent days drawing a map of the cities and the ruins he found there. As he explored, he found art on a rock showing armed men, women, lions, and mythical creatures of all kinds, as well as a type of writing.

The Hittite Empire

Texier's findings inspired many others to explore the region. They discovered thousands of clay tablets detailing the history of people known as the Hittites. Among the earliest inhabitants of Anatolia, they likely came to the area from eastern Europe and central Asia. The town of Bogazkale is on the site of an ancient Hittite town called Hattusa. The oldest tablets found in Bogazkale date back to the seventeenth century BCE. The Hittites

Opposite: **Marching guardians are carved into the walls of a religious building in Hattusa, the capital of the Hittite Empire.**

Ancient and Modern **39**

eventually conquered most of Anatolia and northern Syria and controlled important trade routes through the region. They also developed ironworking skills, helping bring about the Iron Age.

By about 1200 BCE, the Hittite Empire was under threat from all sides. The Assyrians were pushing north from Syria, the Phrygians were moving south from Thrace, and the Sea Peoples were moving along the Mediterranean coast. The empire finally crumbled in about 1193 BCE, and for a time no one group dominated Anatolia. Some of the newcomers settled down; others moved on. The Greeks began establishing cities along the Aegean coast, including Miletus and Ephesus.

Changing Hands

By the sixth century BCE, the Achaemenid Empire of Persia, in what is now Iran, conquered Anatolia. The Greeks continued to have a strong influence in the west, and they eventually revolted against the Persians. The Achaemenid Empire was weakening, and when the young and determined Alexander the Great, a Greek Macedonian, brought his army to the region in 334 BCE,

Ancient Turkey

— Present-day Turkey

☐ Hittite Empire, 1346 BCE

☐ Achaemenid Empire, 331 BCE

☐ Empire of Alexander, 323 BCE

■ Roman Empire, 120 CE

Deep Below the Surface

Scuba diving in the turquoise waters of the Aegean Sea off Turkey is a popular activity among tourists. Some people are hoping to get a good look at sea creatures. Others are searching for shipwrecks.

During World War I, battles raged off the Turkish coast, and hundreds of boats and ships sank to the dark ocean bottom. So far, determined divers have found more than two hundred wrecks. Many of these vessels have become encrusted by sea life and provide a home to everything from conger eels to lobsters.

But some scuba divers in the Aegean have discovered far older wrecks. In 1982, a Turkish diver discovered a 3,300-year-old wreck of a trade ship off Uluburun, a point in southwestern Turkey. Dating from the fourteenth century BCE, it is the world's oldest shipwreck ever found.

Between 1982 and 1994, professional divers examined the wreck, diving more than 22,400 times. The wreck was full of trade goods and other artifacts. The ship carried cargo from seven different cultures. Brought to the surface and put on display for the world to see were a wide array of items, including ebony logs, elephant tusks, hippopotamus teeth, tortoise shells, ostrich eggshells, and amber beads. Other cargo included fishing gear, tools, pottery, and glass, as well as traces of nuts, figs, olives, and spices.

he was able to seize control of Anatolia and Thrace. After this, Greek influence began spreading across Anatolia and was no longer limited to coastal regions. New settlements were established and the Greek language became more common. Alexander's reign was brief, however. After his death in 323 BCE, a number of smaller empires fought for control of Anatolia.

Turkey's Wonders of the World

Turkey is the proud home of two of the Seven Wonders of the Ancient World, fabulous monuments from the eastern Mediterranean region. They are the Temple of Artemis (below) in Ephesus and the Mausoleum of Halicarnassus (right) in Bodrum. While there is little left of either site, they are important parts of Turkey's rich history.

The Temple of Artemis was built in the mid-sixth century BCE to honor Artemis, the Greek goddess of the moon. The temple once included 127 columns standing 60 feet (18 m) high. Inside the temple were sculptures and paintings of gods and goddesses. In 356 BCE, the

temple was set on fire and most of it was destroyed. Alexander the Great had it rebuilt, but it was destroyed once again in 262 CE. The temple was discovered in 1869, and excavations began. Sadly, little of the temple remained. Only a single column stands today.

The Mausoleum of Halicarnassus in Bodrum was built as a very elaborate tomb for Mausolus, a governor in the Persian Empire. The tomb stood over 130 feet (40 m) high. Statues of Greek gods filled the courtyard, and stone warriors guarded the four corners of the building. Thirty-six marble columns supported a pyramid-shaped roof. An earthquake damaged the mausoleum in the thirteenth century, and over time the fallen stones were taken to use in the construction of other sites. Today, little remains of the original structure except shattered columns and stone walls. The ancient wonder had a lasting effect, however: it is the origin of the word *mausoleum*, meaning any aboveground tomb.

Eventually, in the second century BCE the Romans became involved in the conflict, and by the first century BCE, they ruled all of Anatolia. Under their control, Anatolia remained at peace for several centuries.

In 330 CE, Roman emperor Constantine I moved his capital from Rome to Byzantium, renaming the city Constantinople. In the early years of Christianity, the religion had spread across much of Anatolia. Constantine had also become a Christian, and Constantinople was the center of the Orthodox Church.

Constantine (below) was proclaimed the Roman emperor in 306 in York, England, after his father, Constantius I, was killed in battle with the local Pict people.

The World Below

A lot of history lies under the ancient streets of Istanbul. Over the centuries, buildings have been constructed on top of ruins on top of rubble. Under Istanbul today are the remains of palaces and mosques, ports and stables. There are also dozens of cisterns, large rooms for holding water. One of the most extraordinary is known as the Basilica Cistern. This vast room is 469 feet (143 m) long—longer than four football fields end to end. Its roof is held up by 336 columns that rise out of the water. The effect is elegant and mysterious.

The Basilica Cistern was built under Emperor Justinian I in 532. It eventually fell out of use and was all but forgotten until the 1500s, when officials discovered that some people were fishing by lowering buckets through their floors. Today, visitors can walk down a set of stairs in the old city of Istanbul and experience an eerie piece of the past.

As the seat of an empire, Constantinople grew quickly. The city was wealthy, and grand buildings and churches were constructed. By the time Justinian I took the throne in 527 CE, Constantinople was home to more than half a million people.

Emperor Justinian I (center) was considered an ambitious leader who was concerned about the well-being of his people. He is best remembered for revising Roman law and making it more orderly.

The Best of the Byzantine

The Hagia Sophia, or the Church of the Holy Wisdom, is a cathedral in Istanbul. The spectacular structure was built on the order of the Byzantine emperor between 532 and 537 CE. Many people consider it the world's greatest Byzantine building. It was built on the site of two earlier Byzantine churches, each of which had burned to the ground and were located on the site of an ancient temple.

Supporting a huge main dome, this nearly square building was the largest cathedral in the world for nearly a thousand years. The interior was covered in shimmering, detailed mosaics—images made by putting together small pieces of stone or glass. The mosaics showed Jesus, other religious figures, and Byzantine leaders. Today, only a few of these mosaics remain.

Following the Ottoman conquest of Constantinople in 1453, the building was turned into a mosque. Minarets were added and large disks with Arabic writing were hung from the walls. The grand building has been a museum since 1935.

Anatolia was also changing. New people migrated into Anatolia. In the tenth and eleventh centuries, Slavs came from southeastern Europe and Armenians and Syrians came from the south. In the eleventh century the Seljuq Turks arrived from central Asia. They defeated Byzantine forces in 1071 and gained control of central and eastern Anatolia. Over time, the Seljuqs' Turkish language and Muslim religion became more common across Anatolia. Still, many Greeks, Armenians, and Assyrians continued to speak their own languages and practice Christianity.

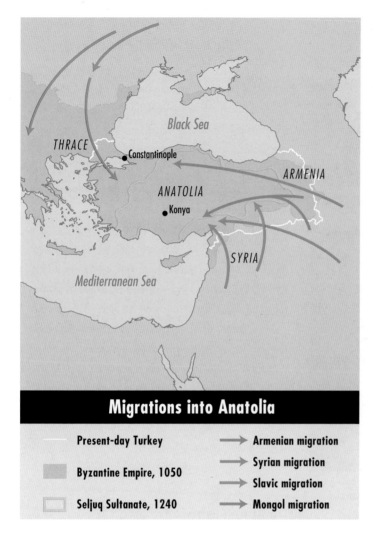

Migrations into Anatolia

—— Present-day Turkey	→ Armenian migration
▓ Byzantine Empire, 1050	→ Syrian migration
☐ Seljuq Sultanate, 1240	→ Slavic migration
	→ Mongol migration

Enter the Ottomans

In the 1200s, the Mongols, people from central Asia, invaded Anatolia, undermining the Seljuqs' power. With the end of the Seljuq Empire, *beyliks*, smaller regions ruled by princes, became the dominant force in Anatolia. One of the *beys*, or princes, was named Osman. He began attacking Byzantine regions, and by about 1300 controlled part of northwestern Anatolia. His son Orhan I followed in his footsteps. As he and his successors continued to expand their realm, the Ottoman Empire was born.

In 1453, the Ottomans conquered Constantinople, renamed it Istanbul, and made it their capital. For the next two centuries, the Ottoman Empire grew and thrived. The Ottomans conquered other lands, including Syria, Egypt, Hungary, the Balkans in southeastern Europe, and almost all of the Middle East. Their ships ruled the Mediterranean Sea, the Black Sea, and the Red Sea, which separates Africa and Asia.

The empire reached its greatest extent under Suleyman the Magnificent, the sultan who ruled from 1520 to 1566.

To the City

The name *Istanbul* comes from the Greek *Eis tin Poli*, which means "To the City." This name arose because Byzantine Greeks referred to Constantinople as *Poli*, or "the City."

During his reign, the Ottomans spread across northern Africa and took Baghdad, in what is now Iraq. They twice attacked Vienna, Austria, but could not conquer the city. Besides being a great military leader, Suleyman was also a great patron of the arts. He supported poets and architects, such as Mimar Sinan, who brought Ottoman architecture to new heights in buildings such as the Selimiye Mosque in Edirne. All around the empire, grand fortresses, palaces, bridges, and mosques were constructed.

Suleyman the Magnificent reigned for forty-six years, longer than any other Ottoman sultan.

Decline and Change

The Ottoman Empire faltered in the years after Suleyman because of weak sultans. Meanwhile, European nations had discovered new trade routes, so they were no longer dependent on those that went through the Middle East. The Ottoman economy suffered. By the eighteenth century, the Ottomans were losing territory. They tried making changes to halt their losses, including reorganizing their military and improving their educational system, but nothing worked. By the nineteenth century, as more and more territories became independent from the Ottoman Empire, Europeans called the empire "the Sick Man of Europe."

The empire adopted its first constitution in 1876 as part of its attempt to modernize. Under the constitution, the sultan still held all power, but he was assisted by a parliament. The constitution lasted only two years before Sultan Abdulhamid II dissolved parliament and ruled through fear.

By the time the nineteenth century was coming to an end, a growing number of Turkish students and military leaders were tired of Abdulhamid's control. These Young Turks, as they were called, held secret meetings and, in 1908, forced the restoration of the constitution. The following year, Abdulhamid stepped down.

When World War I began, the Ottomans entered the war on the side of the Central powers, which included Germany, against the Allies, which included the United Kingdom, Russia, and the United States. During the war, the Russian

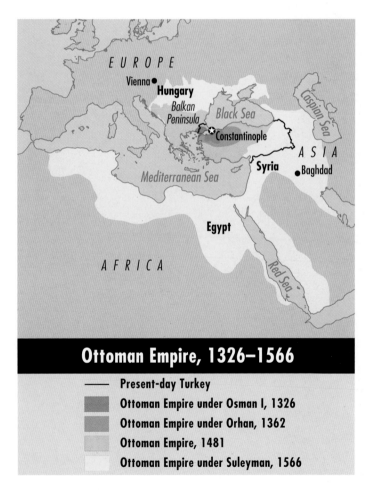

Ottoman Empire, 1326–1566

— Present-day Turkey

■ Ottoman Empire under Osman I, 1326

■ Ottoman Empire under Orhan, 1362

■ Ottoman Empire, 1481

□ Ottoman Empire under Suleyman, 1566

Young Turks wave Turkish flags in 1908. The Young Turks believed in Turkish nationalism and wanted to modernize their land.

army began moving into eastern Anatolia. The Ottoman government feared the Christian Armenians in Anatolia would side with the Christian Russians, so the Ottomans deported or killed an estimated six hundred thousand Armenians. This is known as the Armenian genocide.

Creating Turkey

After the Allies defeated the Central powers in 1918, British, French, Italian, and Greek troops were sent to occupy

Greek-speaking people from Turkey wait to board ships that will take them to Greece, a country they had never lived in. Under the Treaty of Lausanne, most Greek-speaking people had to leave Turkey.

Istanbul. This led to a rise in Turkish nationalism. Although what remained of the Ottoman government was willing to cooperate with the occupiers, the nationalists were not.

The Turkish national movement was led by a military hero named Mustafa Kemal. He and the sultan battled for power as each man fought to be the legitimate leader of the government. In 1920, the new Grand National Assembly met and elected Kemal president. A treaty the Allies had forced on the Ottoman Empire at the end of the war gave parts of Anatolia and Thrace to Greece. Under Kemal's leadership, Turkish forces pushed out the Greeks. Other occupying forces also withdrew.

In 1923, the Treaty of Lausanne set Turkey's current borders and recognized the Republic of Turkey as the lawful government of the nation. The Ottoman sultanate was no more. The treaty required that Greece and Turkey have a population exchange. About 1.3 million Greek-speaking Christians left Turkey for Greece, and about 400,000 Muslims were forced from Greece.

Kemal started modernizing Turkey. He wanted Turkey to have a secular (nonreligious) government. Religious courts were abolished, divorce was made legal, and some religious groups were banned. Women gained the right to vote and to be elected to the assembly. All Turks were also required to adopt a last name. The assembly gave Kemal the name Ataturk, or "Father of the Turks." Although some of his reforms aroused fierce opposition, he continued to push his agenda. Ataturk dominated Turkey until his death in 1938.

Political Turmoil

In the first decades of the Republic of Turkey, the country had only one political party: the Republican People's Party, which is known as CHP after it's name in Turkish. Turkey became a multiparty

Mustafa Kemal Ataturk began his career as an officer in the Ottoman army. He became a revolutionary and a statesman, and is considered the founder of the Republic of Turkey.

Adnan Menderes served as the Turkish prime minister throughout the 1950s. Menderes was more open to traditional ways of life and conservative Islam than Mustafa Kemal Ataturk had been.

democracy in 1946, when the Democrat Party (DP) was founded. The DP took control of the Grand National Assembly in 1950 and led the country for the rest of the decade. Although the economy had grown by 1953, harvests were bad and prices were increasing rapidly. As people began to clamor for change, the government responded by clamping down on dissent. The government prosecuted some journalists for insulting Turkey,

outlawed some political parties, and limited teachers in their freedom. The DP also began relaxing some of the restrictions on religious activity. By 1960, the government was cracking down on the CHP, and students had taken to the streets to demonstrate.

Many army officers feared the rising influence of Islamism and did not believe that the DP was committed to Turkey's secularism. In May 1960, the army carried out a coup, taking over the government and arresting the DP leaders. A new constitution was written, and civilian rule returned by late 1961.

Thousands of Turks gathered in Istanbul to celebrate the military coup that overthrew Prime Minister Adnan Menderes in 1960.

Ancient and Modern **53**

Soldiers seal off a road in Ankara during a military coup in 1980. General Kenan Evren, who led the coup, went on to become the president of Turkey.

In the 1960s and 1970s, Turkey had a series of weak governments. Political violence was also on the rise. Some of the violence was in southeastern Anatolia, where large numbers of Kurdish ethnic people live. Some of the Kurds wanted greater freedom; others wanted to separate from Turkey entirely.

Amid the growing turmoil, the army stepped in again, carrying out coups in 1971 and 1980. In both cases, army officers worried about the growing violence and feared growing Islamism.

Recent Times

In the aftermath of the 1980 coup, a new constitution was written and the country seemed to grow more stable. The economy flourished in the mid-1980s. During the Persian Gulf

War in 1991, Turkey supported the United States by shutting down Iraq's oil pipeline through Turkey, as well as giving the U.S forces use of Turkish airfields. Although this was hard on the country's economy, it showed Turkey's support of America. In the years since, the country has continued to grow wealthier, more industrial, and more urban.

Recent years have also seen a growth in the power of Islamists in government, especially under the leadership of

American troops provided supplies to Kurdish refugee camps in Turkey in the aftermath of the Persian Gulf War of 1991.

In 2013, thousands of
Kurds filled the streets of
Diyarbakir in southeastern
Turkey in support of a
peaceful solution to the
Kurdish conflict.

Recep Tayyip Erdogan, who became prime minister in 2003.
One of the biggest issues during his time in office has been
whether women should be allowed to wear head scarves
in universities and other public buildings. Many observant
Muslim women cover their hair. But the secular Turkish government has long opposed religious expression in government
buildings, so it banned the wearing of head scarves there. The

ban on wearing head scarves in universities was lifted in 2011, and the ban on female workers wearing head scarves ended in 2013. While many people agree with these changes, some Turks believe Erdogan is too religiously conservative.

The conflict between the Turks and the Kurds has eased somewhat in recent years. Turkey has moved to find a peaceful solution for coexisting with the Kurdish minority. In 2013, Kurdish separatists agreed to a cease-fire with Turkey. The long conflict has killed about forty thousand people, mostly Kurds. Everyone in Turkey remains hopeful that the peace will hold.

See It on YouTube

In 2007, Internet users in Turkey suddenly lost access to YouTube. The government decided to block the site because there were videos on it that criticized and ridiculed Ataturk, the founder of the country. YouTube is only one of almost eight thousand Web sites that have been banned in Turkey. The government explains that about 90 percent of those sites are violent and abusive, while another 10 percent or so insult Ataturk, and 1 percent is banned for "other reasons."

In late 2010, the YouTube ban was lifted when ten controversial videos about Ataturk were officially removed. While Internet users are pleased about the change, many of them think it is not enough. "It's a face-saving solution," says Mustafa Akgul, president of Internet Technologies Association. "It did not address the main problems, the main questions of Internet censorship."

CHAPTER 5

Governing the Republic

SINCE TURKEY BECAME A REPUBLIC IN 1923, THE government has attempted to keep religion and the state separate. Although the population of the country is almost entirely Sunni Muslim, those in power have typically believed that it is important that religious ideas not be behind the actions the government takes or does not take. This principle of secularism has been a difficult one to maintain—even more so now with a president and prime minister who clearly demonstrate their religious beliefs.

Opposite: **The Turkish Grand National Assembly meets in a modern building in Ankara.**

Three Branches

Since 1923, the structure of Turkey's government has undergone little change. Its most current constitution was adopted in 1982.

Turkey's National Government

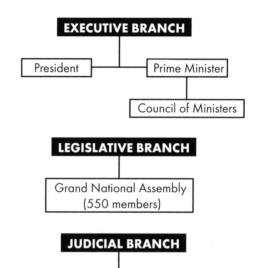

EXECUTIVE BRANCH

President — Prime Minister

Council of Ministers

LEGISLATIVE BRANCH

Grand National Assembly
(550 members)

JUDICIAL BRANCH

Constitutional Court — Court of Cassation

A monument to Ataturk stands outside the Grand National Assembly building.

In June 2011, Recep Tayyip Erdogan (upper left) began his third term in office as Turkey's prime minister. He is considered one of the most successful political leaders in the country's history. Some people credit Erdogan with strengthening the country's economy. But some of his critics think he is doing more harm than good. Although he has stated that he believes that Turkey should have a secular government, he has made some decisions that contradict this. He has made announcements about how many children families should have, passed laws restricting the time and place alcohol can be sold, and spoken against coed dormitories and off-campus housing at state universities. In 2013, Turkey saw large demonstrations over Erdogan's plan to turn an Istanbul park into a shopping mall. Many people who took to the streets (lower left) saw this as an example of his authoritarian style—making decisions without concern for what the people want.

The president is the head of state and leader of the executive branch. He or she is commander in chief of the armed forces and presides over the Grand National Assembly. Elected by popular vote, the president serves a five-year term and can be reelected once. Abdullah Gul has been president since 2007.

The head of government is the prime minister, who is chosen by the assembly. Turkey's prime minister is Recep Tayyip Erdogan, who has held the office since 2003. The prime minister is the leader of the assembly. He or she also selects the members of the cabinet, called the Council of Ministers. The cabinet has the job of overseeing various departments, such as finance, foreign affairs, and culture and tourism.

National Anthem

The lyrics to Turkey's national anthem, "Istiklal Marsi" ("Independence March"), were written by Mehmet Akif Ersoy in 1921. The music was written by Osman Zeki Ungor nine years later. It was officially adopted in 1921. Although the song has a total of ten verses, only the first two are commonly sung.

Turkish lyrics

Korkma, sonmez bu safaklarda yuzen al sancak
Sonmeden yurdumun ustunde tuten en son ocak.
O benim milletimin yildizidir, parlayacak!
O benimdir, o benim milletimindir ancak!
Catma, kurban olayim, cehreni ey nazli hilal!
Kahraman irkima bir gul...ne bu siddet, bu celal?
Sana olmaz dokulen kanlarimiz sonra helal.
Hakkidir, Hakka tapan milletimin istiklal.

English translation

Fear not, the crimson flag, waving in these dawns will
   never fade
Before the last hearth that is burning in my nation vanishes.
That is my nation's star, it will shine;
That is mine, it belongs solely to my nation.
Oh coy crescent do not frown for I am ready to sacrifice
   myself for you!
Please smile upon my heroic nation, why that anger, why
   that rage?
If you frown, our blood shed for you will not be worthy.
Freedom is the right of my nation who worships God and
   seeks what is right.

The Grand National Assembly is the legislative branch of the Turkish government. The assembly includes 550 members, who are elected according to a system of proportional representation. This means that the number of seats each party has in the assembly is the same as the percentage of votes that party received. In Turkey, a party must win at least 10 percent of the vote to get seats in the assembly. Members of the assembly are elected to four-year terms. Turkish people must

Supporters of the Republican People's Party rally in Ankara in 2011. The party, which favors secularism in Turkey, is currently the nation's second-largest party and the main opposition to Turkey's Islamist leaders.

National Flag

On June 5, 1936, the bright red and white flag of Turkey was officially adopted. Known as the *ay yildiz*, or "moon star," the flag shows a white crescent moon and five-pointed star against a red background. The crescent moon symbolizes Islam, although images of crescent moons were used in the Middle East even before the emergence of Islam. Some historical experts think the moon and stars arose from Greek mythology. The red of the Turkish flag represents the Ottoman Empire.

be at least eighteen years old to vote. The Grand National Assembly is responsible for making laws, accepting treaties,

A woman in Istanbul casts her ballot. Turkey has one of the highest rates of voter turnout in the world. In 2011, 87 percent of eligible voters went to the polls.

and declaring war. If the assembly passes a bill, but the president does not approve it, the bill is returned to the assembly. If the assembly approves it a second time, the bill becomes law.

Turkey has several high courts. The Constitutional Court decides questions of whether laws are legal under the Turkish constitution. The Court of Cassation is the highest criminal court. It reviews the decisions of cases that have been tried in lower courts.

The members of Turkey's Constitutional Court also serve on other high courts.

A President and a Controversy

By the time Abdullah Gul (above left) was elected president in 2007 by a large majority, he had been involved in politics for more than fifteen years. He was elected a member of the Grand National Assembly in 1991 and became prime minister in 2002. Previously, he had been an economics professor at Istanbul University.

Gul is the first strongly Islamist president Turkey has had. Although Turkey is predominantly Muslim, national leaders have kept religion out of government since it became a republic. Having a president who has questioned Turkey's commitment to secularism has worried some Turks. They fear that Gul's religious beliefs will interfere with his presidential decisions. Some also object to the fact that his wife, Hayrunnisa Ozyurt Gul (above right), wears a traditional Muslim head scarf at all times. In Turkey, wearing this head scarf was long banned in government buildings. The head scarf is a symbol of faith, and one that many believe should not be displayed by a spouse of the president. More Turks, however, share Gul's deeply held religious views and social conservatism.

Regional Government

Turkey is divided into eighty-one provinces, each headed by a governor. These provinces, in turn, are split up into hundreds of counties, districts, municipalities, and villages. Each district has its own mayor, while villages are watched over by chiefs.

Welcome to Ankara

The people who lived in Ankara a century ago would never recognize the city it has become today. When Ataturk made it the national capital in 1923, it was not a thriving city like it is today. At the time, Ankara had a population of only about 35,000. Today, with 4.6 million residents, Ankara is the second-largest city in the nation, after Istanbul.

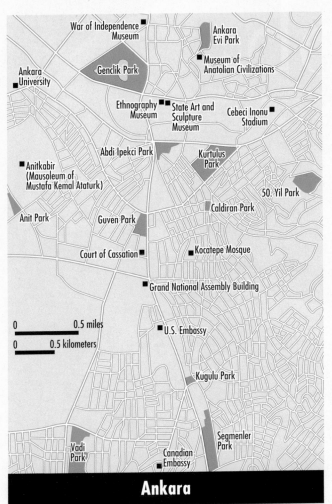

War of Independence Museum
Ankara Evi Park
Museum of Anatolian Civilizations
Ankara University
Genclik Park
Ethnography Museum
State Art and Sculpture Museum
Cebeci Inonu Stadium
Abdi Ipekci Park
Kurtulus Park
Anitkabir (Mausoleum of Mustafa Kemal Ataturk)
50. Yil Park
Caldiran Park
Anit Park
Guven Park
Court of Cassation
Kocatepe Mosque
Grand National Assembly Building
0   0.5 miles
0   0.5 kilometers
U.S. Embassy
Kugulu Park
Vadi Park
Canadian Embassy
Segmenler Park

Ankara

Ankara is modern in many ways, with soaring skyscrapers, bustling businesses, and a sophisticated underground railway system. At the same time, it is the site of many historical mosques, ruins, and monuments, plus galleries and museums that honor the country's rich culture. The city boasts Roman ruins that date back to the third century, but it is also known for its new buildings, such as the Kocatepe Mosque, which was finished in 1987. It is the city's largest mosque. Major museums in Ankara include the Ethnography Museum, which features displays about carpet making, woodworking, wedding traditions, and much more, and the Museum of Anatolian Civilizations (above), which contains artifacts from archaeological sites throughout Turkey.

CHAPTER 6

On the Job

EFORE ATATURK CHANGED THE COUNTRY dramatically, most of the people in Turkey lived as farmers. After the sweeping changes of the "Father of the Turks," more and more people left the countryside and headed for new careers in the cities. Whereas in the 1920s, Turkey had only hundreds of factories, within a few decades after that time, it had thousands.

The number of people involved in agriculture continues to drop. Currently, about 25 percent of the labor force works in farming. These farmers work hard to keep Turkey the top world supplier of figs, apricots, hazelnuts, and raisins.

Opposite: **Turkey is the world's fourth-largest producer of tomatoes. In 2011, Turkish farmers grew more than 11 million metric tons of tomatoes.**

Follow the Money

In 2005, Turkish money lost a lot of zeroes. Six zeroes were dropped from each denomination of the Turkish lira to make the Yeni (meaning new) Turkish lira. This made the money more practical. It was much easier for people to use bills in increments of ones, tens, and hundreds than it was to deal with millions, billions, trillions, and even quadrillions. Of course, the changes were confusing at first. All stores had to post signs showing the old and new rates so that shoppers would have the right amount of money for what they wanted to buy.

Four years later, in 2009, the Turkish currency was changed again. Now Turkish bills look far more like the euro notes used throughout much of Europe. Each denomination has a different dominant color. All Turkish bills have an image of Ataturk on the front, and an image of a prominent Turk on the back. For instance, the 10 Turkish lira note is mainly red and on the back is a portrait of Cahit Arf, an influential mathematician.

Turkish banknotes come in denominations of 5, 10, 20, 50, 100, and 200 lira. Each Turkish lira is divided into 100 kurus. Coins come in values of 1, 5, 10, 25, and 50 kurus, and 1 lira. In 2014, 1 Turkish lira equaled 45 cents, and 1 U.S. dollar equaled 2.24 lira.

From the Land

The family farm is still alive in Turkey. Most Turkish farms are small, averaging only about 15 acres (6 ha). Together, this farmland accounts for about one-third of the land in the nation.

Three-quarters of the agricultural land is used to produce vegetables, such as cucumbers, eggplants, peppers, onions, potatoes, and sugar beets. Fruit thrives in the warm climates. Crops include figs, sour cherries, apricots, apples, bananas, and kiwis. Cotton, tea, and tobacco are also important crops, as are lentils, chickpeas, pumpkins, and almonds. Farmers grow a variety of grain, including barley, corn, and wheat. Some of the country's most fertile land is found along the coast. Many of these farms produce olive and sunflower oils, or use the land to raise livestock. Large numbers of cattle, sheep, goats, and water buffalo are raised in Turkey.

The country also grows many flowers for sale, including crocuses, lilies, and the national flower, tulips. About one-quarter of the roses in the world come from Turkey. These roses are exported throughout the world, along with rose oil, called *attar*, which is used for perfume and in making rose water.

What Turkey Grows, Makes, and Mines

AGRICULTURE (2010)

Wheat	19,660,000 metric tons
Sugar beets	17,942,000 metric tons
Tomatoes	10,052,000 metric tons

MANUFACTURING

Steel (2011)	34,100,000 metric tons
Clothing (2006)	US$14,000,000,000 in exports
Motor vehicles (2012)	1,072,339 produced

MINING (2009)

Chromite	1,574,000 metric tons
Magnesite	861,000 metric tons
Copper	105,000 metric tons

Resources

Mixed cereals, livestock	Ag Silver	Cu Copper	Mag Magnesite
Cash crops	Au Gold	Fe Iron	NG Natural gas
Forest	Bx Bauxite	Fz Fertilizer	Pb Lead
Pasture livestock	Cem Cement	Hg Mercury	Petroleum
Nomadic livestock herding	Cr Chromite	Lig Lignite	Zn Zinc
Nonagricultural land			

Deep in the Ground

The economic richness of Turkey is not only from what it can grow on the ground, but from what can be found under the ground as well. Dozens of kinds of minerals are commercially mined in Turkey. One of the most important minerals found in Turkey is copper. The country also produces large amounts of magnesite, which is used in the production of rubber, chemicals, and other goods; and chromite, which is used in making stainless steel. Turkey also mines iron, lead, zinc, and bauxite.

Manufacturing

Today, industry accounts for more than a quarter of the Turkish economy. The nation produces clothing and other

Every day, as many as two million people cross from the Asian side of Istanbul to the European side. Until 2013, this trip required either driving or taking a train trip over a bridge across the Bosporus. Now, however, people can cross the Bosporus in an undersea tunnel, 200 feet (60 m) below the sea's surface. Known as the Marmaray Project, the tracks cover 8.5 miles (13.6 km). To get from one continent to the other via the tunnel takes only about four minutes.

Building this tunnel was dangerous because of Turkey's high risk of earthquakes. It was built only about 10 miles (16 km) from an active fault. Being underground during an earthquake is dangerous, but not because the ground will collapse from the shaking. In fact, being deep in the ground protects a person from the shaking. The real risk is what happens to the wet, sandy soil during an earthquake. It gets soft—so soft it almost turns into liquid. This process can make the tunnel begin to float up through the ground.

To prevent the chance of this happening, builders injected grout, a type of cement, into the ground near the tunnel to make it more stable. In addition, the tunnel has been built in eleven separate sections. This keeps it flexible, so it can move as needed without breaking if the earth begins to quake.

The rail system cost more than $4.5 billion to build. At the opening ceremony of the tunnel in 2013, Prime Minister Recep Erdogan said that the train "connects history and future, past and future; as well as connecting continents, Marmaray connects people, nations, and countries."

In 2011, the Global Summit of Women met in Istanbul. One reason this city was chosen is because so few Turkish women are in the workforce. Although approximately half of Turkish women enter the labor market when they are young, most quit after getting married. Only about 29 percent of the women in Turkey have jobs outside the home, compared to 57 percent of women in the United States. "Turkish women participate in [the workforce] in large numbers—no matter what their level of education—prior to marriage, but end up leaving their jobs upon marriage and having children," explains Ipek Ilkkaracan, a professor of economics at Istanbul Technical University. Some women do not return to work because they struggle to find adequate and affordable child care. Others report having to deal with harassment.

textiles, chemicals, foods and beverages, and motor vehicles. It is also the largest steel producer in the Middle East and a major producer of televisions and other electronic products.

Many of these products are shipped to other countries for sale. Turkey's top exports include food, textiles, metal, and transport equipment. It trades primarily with Germany, Iraq, Iran, the United Kingdom, the United Arab Emirates, Russia, Italy, and France. In addition, Turkey imports machinery, chemicals, fuels, and transport equipment from Russia, Germany, China, the United States, Italy, and Iran.

Come and Visit

In 2012, more than thirty-six million people from all over the world visited Turkey as tourists. This small country has

Sightseeing in Turkey is a normal activity for most tourists, but having one of the stops be a city landfill is unusual. However, a number of people are stopping in Ankara to look at the Mamak Landfill. Why? Because this site operates using innovative techniques that make the disposal of trash more effective and efficient.

At one time, the Mamak Landfill was a source of embarrassment for Turkey. Sitting next to a highway near the airport, it looked awful and smelled even worse. It produced huge amounts of methane, a gas that is dangerous to people and to the environment.

Today, the landfill has become a source of pride and an example to the rest of the world of what is possible. At this landfill, trash is sorted, and the methane it produces is converted into energy, which is used to power greenhouses. Rather than polluting the environment, the methane is turned into heat to grow tomatoes.

In addition, Mamak has created a number of jobs for people who had once fought to survive by working as scavengers in the landfill. In the past, people regularly sifted through trash in search of items they could sell or recycle. They were at great risk of being injured or becoming sick. But now, more than thirty local people have been hired to work for the recycling plant.

become one of the world's top vacation destinations. Many tourists arrive from Europe, but large numbers also come from

Workers build cars at a plant in Bursa. Turkey manufactures more than one million motor vehicles every year.

Tourists wade in natural pools fed by hot springs at a site called Pamukkale, which means "cotton castle" in Turkish. Each year, more than seven hundred thousand people visit Pamukkale.

the Middle East, Russia, and elsewhere in Asia. The effect of all these visitors is clear in the city's transportation systems. Turkey has ninety-eight airports and twenty heliports. Whereas once most of its roads were unpaved, currently more than 90 percent of its 240,000 miles (386,000 km) of roadways are paved. In addition, Turkey has 7,461 miles (12,007 km)

of railways and 750 miles (1,200 km) of waterways. Tourist-related services in Turkey reached US$25 billion in 2011, and only seem to keep climbing.

An elevated highway snakes through the Turkish hills.

How Much Does It Cost?

How much does food cost in Turkey compared to the United States? Here are some average prices for items in 2013 from Istanbul.

Item	In Turkey	In the U.S.
Dozen eggs	4 lira ($1.96)	$2.00
Loaf of bread	1 lira (49¢)	$2.20
1 quart (1 L) of milk	1.75 lira (86¢)	$1.00
11 ounce (330 ml) of soda	2 lira (98¢)	$1.50

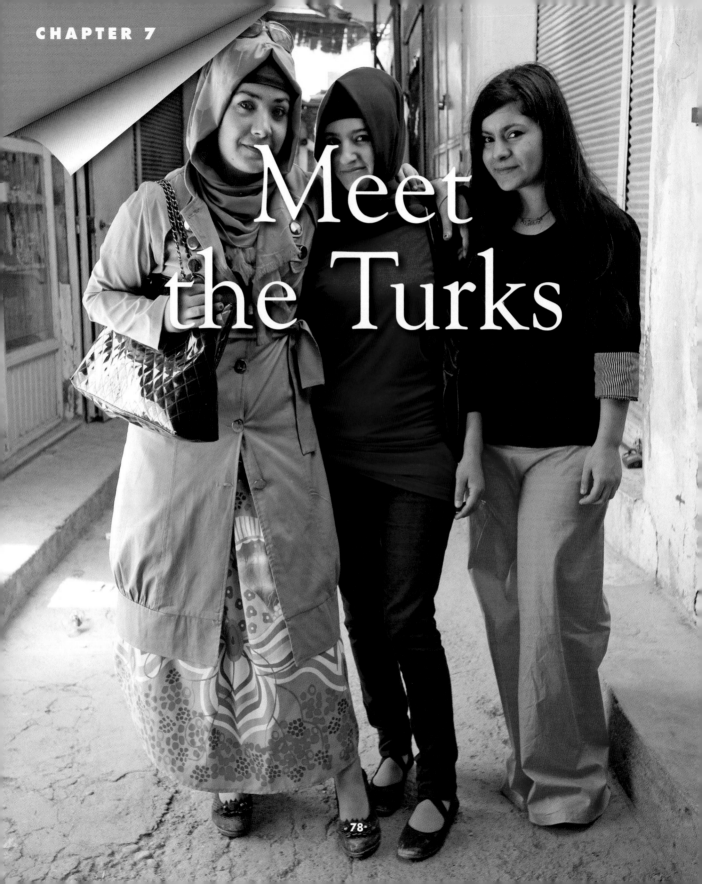

CHAPTER 7

Meet the Turks

N 1927, THE FIRST OFFICIAL CENSUS WAS TAKEN OF the people of Turkey. The population at the time was 13.6 million. By 2013, more than 76.7 million people lived in the country. Even as Turkey's population has grown, other population trends have shifted. For a long time, Turkey was a country with a high birthrate and a relatively young population. Today, however, the average Turkish woman has only two children, and improved health care has resulted in longer lives. Turkish people can now expect to live seventy-three years. As a result of these trends, the number of Turkish people age sixty-five and older is growing at a faster rate than any other age group.

Opposite: **College students in Mardin, in southeastern Turkey.**

In the Cities

Seven of Turkey's cities have populations of one million or more, with the largest being Istanbul. About 18 percent of

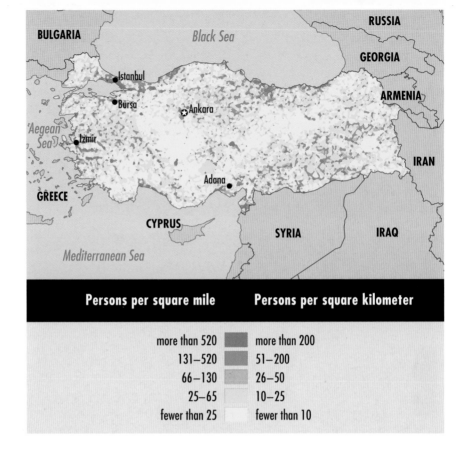

Persons per square mile		Persons per square kilometer	
more than 520		more than 200	
131–520		51–200	
66–130		26–50	
25–65		10–25	
fewer than 25		fewer than 10	

Population of Major Cities (2012 est.)

Istanbul	13,710,512
Ankara	4,630,735
Izmir	3,401,994
Bursa	1,983,880
Adana	1,636,220

Who Lives in Turkey? (2008 est.)

Turks	70–75%
Kurds	16%
Other	7–12%

the country's population lives in Istanbul, and experts believe that, in the future, this will only continue to grow. The nation's fastest-growing city is expected to be Antalya, thanks to its combination of agriculture, industry, and tourism.

Approximately 71.5 percent of Turkey's population lives in the cities and towns, while the rest lives in rural areas. Unemployment is often a serious problem in the rural areas, particularly in the southeast. This drives people into the cities in search of work. At times, the newcomers to the cities have not been able to find jobs and homes. Sometimes people have moved to neighboring countries or as far away as Canada and Australia in order to find jobs.

The People of Turkey

Roughly three-quarters of the people in Turkey consider themselves ethnically Turkish. Turks are a mixture of Slavs, Greeks, Armenians, Kurds, and the Seljuq Turks who arrived in the region in the eleventh century.

Today, about thirteen million Kurds live in Turkey, making them the nation's largest minority group. In the past, Kurds lived largely as nomads, herding sheep and goats through the highlands of Asia. After the collapse of the Ottoman Empire, the Kurds were treated badly, and the Turkish government outlawed the use of their language and their traditional clothing. For decades, the Kurds have fought to get these rights back. It was not until 2012 that any schools were permitted to teach the language. A number of Kurds would like to establish their own state, separate from Turkey, but so far this plan has not moved forward. Much violence has broken out over this issue.

Other people in Turkey include Arabs, Armenians, and Greeks. Most Arabs live near the border with Syria, while Armenians and Greeks live near Istanbul.

The highest concentrations of Turkish Kurds are in the eastern and southeastern parts of the country.

Until 1934, most of the people living in Turkey did not have surnames, or last names. In 1934, Ataturk passed the Surname Act, requiring all citizens to have a last name. The most common last names in the country are Yilmaz (meaning: never gives up), Kaya (rock), Demir (iron), Sahin (falcon), and Celik (steel).

Going to School

Turkish students attend school from September to June.

Before Ataturk established the Republic of Turkey in the 1920s and made public education free, the literacy rate in Turkey was under 10 percent. Today, almost 98 percent of Turkish men and 90 percent of women can read and write.

Turkish children are required to attend school for twelve years. School begins at age six. Until 2012, high school was optional, but today it is required. In school, children study subjects including the Turkish language and literature, science, math, history, art, music, and religious culture. They also study one foreign language: English, French, or German. There are two types of high schools. General high schools provide a broad-based education and preparation for college. Technical and vocational high schools prepare students for a career by focusing on a specific field such as agriculture or electronics.

There are 174 universities and other institutions of higher education in Turkey. The oldest university is Istanbul University, which was founded in 1453. It is also the largest university in Turkey, with more than eighty thousand students. Marmara University was founded in 1883 and is the second-largest university in Turkey.

Language

The vast majority of people living in Turkey speak Turkish. Turkish is related to other languages from central Asia and eastern Europe. Over the centuries, Turkish had borrowed many words from Arabic and Persian. Ataturk, the founder of modern Turkey, despised this fact. He wanted to put distance between the Turkey he was trying to establish and the one of the past centuries. One way to do this was to make the past "unreadable" to its people. So in 1928, he insisted that the country switch from using the Arabic alphabet to using a

Arabic writing decorates the tiles at Topkapi Palace in Istanbul.

Learning a Few Turkish Phrases

English	Turkish	Pronunciation
Hello	Merhaba	MEHR-hah-bah
Good-bye	Elveda	el-veh-DAH
How are you?	Nasilsin?	nah-SUL-sun
I am fine	Iyiyim	ee-YI-yim
Thank you	Tesekkur ederim	Tesh-ek-KEWR ed-er-im
Please	Lutfen	LEWT-fen
Yes	Evet	eh-VEHT
No	Hayir	HAH-yuhr

twenty-nine-letter Latin alphabet. Turkey's alphabet today is much like the one used in English, but Turkish words do not contain any *q*'s, *w*'s, or *x*'s, and several letters have two versions, one with an accent mark.

The Turkish alphabet features two versions of several letters, one plain and one with an extra mark above or below the letter that changes the pronunciation. For example, *s* is pronounced as in *sea* and *ş* is pronounced as in *shell*.

SOĞUKÇEŞME
SOKAĞı 1→13
CANKURTARAN MAHALLESİ
FATİH (TN:5)

A woman and her grandson tend a garden in southern Turkey. When this woman was a child, less than a third of Turks could read and write.

Completely changing a language like that is a daunting process that experts predicted would take years. Ataturk did not see it that way. He gave the people six months to make the transition, changing every sign, menu, textbook, and other written material throughout Turkey. It was very difficult and it created a divide between generations who soon lost the ability to communicate clearly with each other.

Turkish is what is known as an agglutinative language. This means that endings to words are added, one by one, to the root of the word. If enough endings are added to a root word, a single word can become a full sentence. For example, look how the word *terbiye*, which means "good manners," changes with additional endings:

good manners	*terbiye*
bad manners	*terbiyesiz*
rudeness	*terbiyesizlik*
their rudeness	*terbiyesizlikleri*
from their rudeness	*terbiyesizliklerinden*
I gather that it was due to their rudeness.	*Terbiyesizliklerindenmis*

Most elementary school children in Turkey attend public school. Less than 1 percent go to private school.

CHAPTER 8

Spiritual Life

MOST PEOPLE IN TURKEY ARE MUSLIM—BY some counts, more than 99 percent. But that does not mean that all Turks have the same attitude toward religion. In a poll in 2007, about 3 percent of Turks identified themselves as nonbelievers. Another 34 percent said they are believers, but they do not perform the religious obligations of Islam. For example, they seldom or never pray. About 54 percent of those polled said they try to fulfill Islam's religious obligations, and another 10 percent said they do fulfill them.

As with other religions, Islam teaches morals and behavior. Muslims are expected to be respectful to their parents, faithful to their spouses, and compassionate to other people. Values such as virtue, charity, and kindness are important to the followers of Islam.

Following the Pillars

Islam is an Arabic word that means a combination of "submission" and "peace." That is the central idea behind the

Opposite: **Selimiye Mosque in Edirne has four slender minarets. Long ago, people would climb these tall towers to announce when it was time to pray. Now, the call to prayer is broadcast from loudspeakers.**

A Prophet to the People

High in the mountain town of Mecca, in western Arabia, in about 570 CE, a baby named Muhammad was born. Muhammad would change the face of world religion. In his youth, he worked as a shepherd, and later as a trader. He earned the nickname El-Amin, or "the one who could be trusted." After becoming a husband and a father, he began fasting and meditating in a mountain cave several weeks a year. He said that while there, he was visited by what he believed was the angel Gabriel. The angel is said to have told Muhammad that he was destined to be a messenger of God—"Allah" in the Arabic language—and a prophet to the people. Until his death in 632, Muhammad shared the revelations that he is said to have received from God, spreading the word of the religion Islam and helping people better understand how they should live their lives.

This beautiful Ottoman Qur'an was made in the fourteenth century.

religion. It preaches the idea of complete submission to God, and kindness, mercy, and forgiveness to others. The tenets of the religion date back to the revelations Muhammad is said to have received from God. These messages were collected

together, becoming the 114 chapters and 6,236 verses of the Qur'an, the holy book of Islam. The verses in the Qur'an form the basis for how observant Muslims live their life, from how and when they should pray to how they spend their money.

Islam has five basic beliefs, or pillars of faith, that all Muslims are expected to follow:

1. The core belief of the religion is summed up in the statement, "There is no god but God, and Muhammad is the

Muslims ritually wash parts of their body before entering a mosque. Most mosques in Turkey have faucets where people can wash.

Turkey's Religious Calendar

The Islamic calendar is eleven days shorter than the Western calendar, so the dates of Muslim holidays change in the Western calendar from year to year.

Mevlid-i Nebi	Celebration of Muhammad's birthday
Regaip Kandili	Celebration of Muhammad's conception
Mirac Kandili	Celebration of the ascent of Muhammad into heaven
Ramadan	Holy month
'Id al-Fitr	Feast celebrating the end of Ramadan
'Id al-Adha	Feast of Abraham's sacrifice of Isaac

messenger of God." Muslims believe that Muhammad was a human messenger sent by God to teach people. The Qur'an also includes stories about Jesus, Adam, Noah, and Moses, whom Muslims also consider messengers, or prophets.

2. Every day, Muslims are to pray at five set times, a process referred to as *namaz*. Before praying, they wash their hands, feet, and face. Then they pray in the direction of Mecca, the city of Muhammad's birth in what is now Saudi Arabia. Five times a day, at every mosque, a call goes out announcing prayer time. Observant

Men pray at Sakirin Mosque in Istanbul. Muslims remove their shoes when they pray.

Muslims stop whatever they are doing to participate, whether they are at home, school, or work.

Turks in Istanbul enjoy picnics after dark during Ramadan.

3. Muslims are to give generously to those in need, either directly or through the mosque they attend. The money is given to the poor within the community.

4. During Ramadan (Ramazan in Turkish), the ninth month in the Islamic year, Muslims should fast—not eat or drink—from sunrise to sundown. They are also expected to exhibit their best behavior during this month. Many restaurants close during those hours and open late.

5. Any Muslim who is physically and financially capable of traveling to Mecca is expected to do so at least once in his or her lifetime.

Turkish Proverbs

You can learn a great deal about a culture by examining some of its most familiar sayings. Consider these Turkish proverbs:

Stretch your legs to the length of your blanket.

You reap whatever you sow.

There is nothing more expensive than what is bought cheaply, and there is nothing cheaper than what is bought expensively.

A pen is sharper than a sword.

A vinegar seller with a smiling face makes more money than a honey seller with a sour face.

A Split in Belief

A religious leader called an imam speaks at a mosque in Istanbul.

A major division within Islam has led to much conflict over the years. When Muhammad died in 632, he did not name a successor, or spiritual heir. His followers argued over the ques-

tion of who would take his place. Some thought it should be Ali, the prophet's cousin, and that group of people became known as the Shi'a, or "faction." Others wanted Muhammad's father-in-law, Abu Bakr, to become leader. They identified themselves as Sunni, which comes from the word for tradition. This division in Islam still exists today. The majority of Muslims, both in Turkey and around the world, are Sunni. In Turkey, Shi'a Muslims probably make up 20 to 30 percent of the population. Most of them belong to a sect called Alevism.

Alevism is a version of Shi'a Islam. Instead of worshipping in mosques, Alevis meet in assembly houses called *cemevis*.

Sufism

Another sect, or group, of Muslims is known as the Sufi. Sufism is a mystical form of Islam that focuses on the inner spirit. Its practitioners are somewhat similar to Buddhist or Christian monks who try to purify themselves to come closer to God. Sufis try to become closer to God by going into a trance state. In Turkey, some Sufis, known as whirling dervishes, enter a trance state by doing a spinning dance. The first dervishes were active in the thirteenth century under the leadership of Turkish poet and philosopher Mevlana Celaleddin-i Rumi. He believed in

As dervishes spin, their skirts spread out in graceful shapes.

religious tolerance and thought that repeated rotating and twirling helped bring a person closer to God. He wrote:

> Come, come, come again,
>   whoever you may be
> Come again even though you
>   may be a pagan or a fire
>   worshipper
> Our center is not one of
>   despair
> Come again, even if you may
>   have
> Violated your vows a hun-
>   dred times, come again.

Wearing long black robes and *sikkes*, tall beige hats, dervishes first kneel and bow. With solemn faces, they drop their robes, revealing white tunics and long white skirts with trousers underneath. They then begin to dance in counter-clockwise circles. A group of men in the Order of Mevlana quietly chant Allah's name as music plays softly. The dancers turn up to two thousand times in fifteen minutes. They raise their right hands upward to receive God's blessings, and lower their left hands downward to send the blessings to earth.

Although this type of dancing was outlawed by Ataturk in 1925, it was revived in 1957 by the Turkish government.

Mevlana Celaleddin-i Rumi lived in the 1200s. His poetry, which describes everyday life as well as expressing love, longing, and ecstasy, remains popular today.

Healing the Mind and Body

He wanted to build a mosque. She wanted to build a hospital. So together, a Turkish couple created a place designed to heal both the mind and the body. In 1229, Mengujukid Emir Ahmet Shah ordered the construction of the Divrigi Great Mosque in a small town in eastern Anatolia. His wife, Melike Turhan Melek, commissioned a hospital to be built on the same grounds. Centuries later, this mosque and hospital combination is a UNESCO World Heritage Site, a list of places of special cultural or physical significance.

The Great Mosque and Hospital of Divrigi is made of yellow stone and is decorated with many carvings of the moon and sun. The mosque is the larger side of the complex, and includes a prayer room with five aisles, and two cupolas, or dome-shaped roofs. The hospital is smaller, with many beautiful, detailed carvings of flowers and geometric designs. In its day, the building was a place for healing the mind through prayer, and the body through medicine.

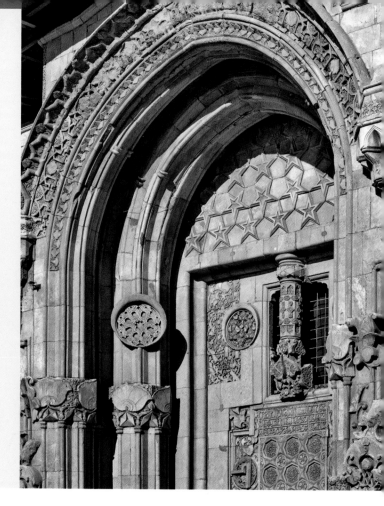

Today, it is considered a cultural event rather than a religious one and is performed primarily for tourists. A few years ago, women began to be allowed to do the ritual dance as well. Rumi's birthday in December is still an important celebration in Turkey, even seven hundred years after his death.

Religion in Turkey	
Muslim	99.8%
Christian/Jewish	0.2%

Christianity

Christianity has a long history in Turkey. Christianity began in lands under the rule of the Roman Empire, which at the time controlled most of Europe and the region around the

Mediterranean. Roman leaders suppressed the new religion until the fourth century, when the Roman emperor Constantine I converted to Christianity himself. He legalized Christian churches and built even more of them, making a Christian state out of the Eastern Roman Empire, which came to be known as the Byzantine Empire. Its capital was Constantinople. For more than one thousand years, Christianity was the more common religion in the Byzantine

Beginning in the fourth century CE, early Christians carved thousands of churches and monks' rooms out of the soft rock in Cappadocia, in central Anatolia. The largest of these churches is known as the Church of the Buckle.

Empire, which ruled the land that is now Turkey. With the arrival of the Seljuq Turks in the eleventh century, Islam began to spread in Antatolia, and when the Ottomans conquered Constantinople in 1453, renaming it Istanbul, Islam became the primary religion of the state. Large numbers of Christians continued to live there, however.

Many of Turkey's Christians left during the population exchange between Turkey and Greece in the early 1920s. Today, the nation's largest Christian population, an estimated forty-five thousand, belongs to the Armenian Apostolic Church. There are also small numbers who belong to the Syriac Orthodox Church, the Greek Orthodox Church, and others.

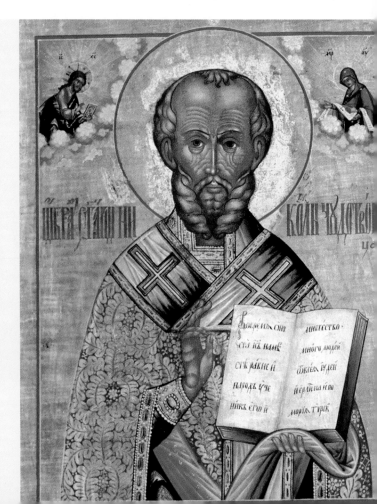

The Birthplace of Santa

Most people picture Santa Claus sitting by the fire in a workshop far in the chilly North Pole, but the man who inspired the character was actually Saint Nicholas from the ancient city Myra, which is now Demre, Turkey. Born in the third century, Nicholas dedicated his life to helping the poor and the sick. He had a reputation for giving gifts to many people and for particularly helping children and sailors. He was even said to creep down chimneys to secretly leave gold for people in need. Years after his death in 343, he was made a saint, and eventually some places in Europe began celebrating his life on the feast day of Saint Nicholas. Over the years, the tradition grew. In the Netherlands, Saint Nicholas became known as Sinterklaas, which in America became Santa Claus.

At Sumela Monastery

High up on the side of the Zigana Mountains outside the city of Trabzon in northeastern Turkey, merging with the trees and passing clouds, is 1,600-year-old Sumela Monastery. The structure was built by Greek priests in 386 CE. After the Ottoman Empire collapsed in 1923 and the Greek Orthodox Christian population of the region was resettled in Greece, Sumela Monastery was abandoned. Today, it is a tourist attraction and museum. Getting to the monastery requires a trip through a lush, green forest. Once at the site, a long stone staircase leads visitors inside, past gray walls covered in paintings called frescoes. In August 2010, the Turkish government allowed a Greek Orthodox mass to be held in the monastery, after an eighty-seven-year ban. Christians from Greece, Russia, Georgia, the United States, and Turkey took part in this religious celebration.

Members of the Armenian Apostolic Church attend a mass in Istanbul.

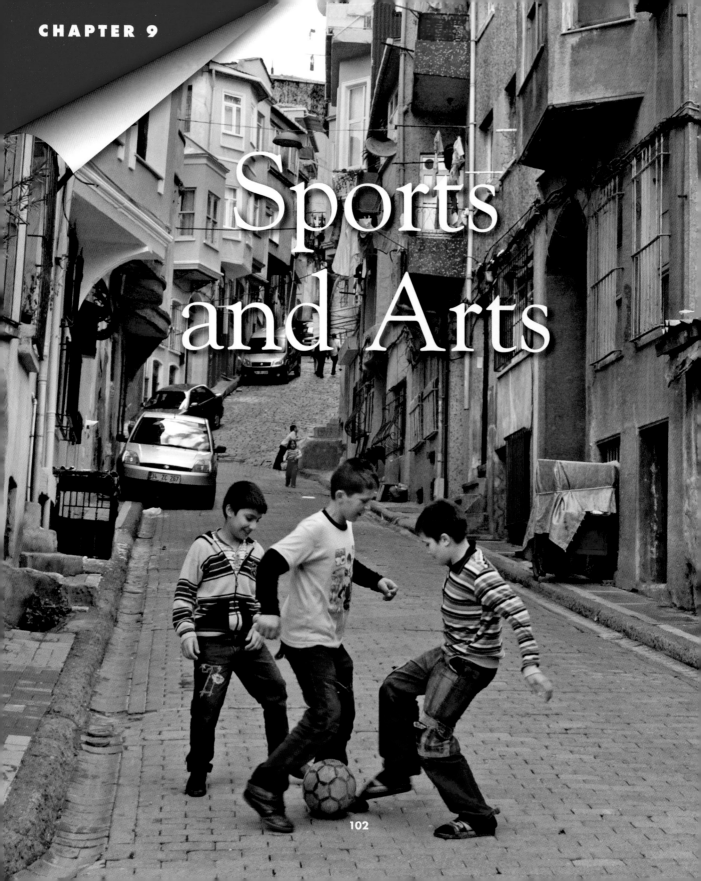

CHAPTER 9

Sports and Arts

THE PEOPLE OF TURKEY LOVE SPORTS—IN FACT, IT is one of the few countries in the world that refers to sports in its constitution. Article 59 states, "The State takes measures to develop the physical and mental health of Turkish citizens of all ages and encourages the spread of sports among the masses. The State protects successful athletes." And, in fact, Turkey has nurtured many successful athletes. Derya Buyukuncu was the first swimmer to compete in six consecutive summer Olympics. Elvan Abeylegesse is a runner who won two medals at the 2008 Olympics and for a time held the world record in the women's 5,000-meter race. One of the nation's most beloved athletes, now retired, is weight lifter Naim Suleymanoglu, known as Pocket Hercules because he stands only 4 feet 11 inches (1.5 m) tall. He won Olympic gold medals in 1988, 1992, and 1996.

Opposite: **Boys play soccer in a narrow street in Istanbul.**

Let's Play!

One of the most popular sports in Turkey is soccer. Fans crowd the stadiums to watch the eighteen teams that play in the top professional league. The league's three most successful teams, Galatasaray, Fenerbahce, and Besiktas, are all based in Istanbul.

Thanks to its long coastline, water sports are popular in Turkey. Tourists especially enjoy the chance to go scuba diving, rafting, canoeing, windsurfing, and kiteboarding. Another fun sport is *jereed*, played with teams throwing javelins from horseback. During the Ottoman era, the game was extremely popular and a means to show power and bravery. In 1826,

Kayaks are an excellent way to explore Turkey's rocky Mediterranean coast.

Camel Wrestling

Many countries are associated with a particular sport. Brazil has soccer, the United States has football, and the United Kingdom has cricket. In the Aegean region of Turkey, the sport is . . . camel wrestling! Each year in the town of Selcuk, the Camel Wrestling Championship is held. For each bout, two big, strong camels are led into the middle of a dusty ring. On their backs are jangling bells, brightly colored rugs, and carved saddles. The animals' owners are inside the arena with them, encouraging the animals to push and shove each other.

The biggest problem with camel wrestling is getting the creatures to actually battle each other. For the most part, camels are not fighters. To help encourage them, contests are held during mating season and a female camel is paraded by to inspire pushing and leaning. (And spitting! A camel that is feeling irritable tends to do a lot of spitting and drooling.) The first camel that is pushed to the side or knocked over, or that just gives up and walks away from the skirmish within a ten-minute time limit, loses. Sometimes both camels seem to decide the hard work is not worth it and walk away together.

the game was outlawed because it was deemed too dangerous. Since then, it is played only with much lighter, safer javelins, and is commonly played only at special occasions such as weddings or local fairs.

Performing Arts

The Turks' love for entertainment goes beyond playing and watching sports. The people love music of all types. Ankara is home to an international music festival, and Istanbul has

Oil Up!

Some people call grease wrestling the national sport of Turkey. In this messy sport, the wrestlers cover themselves in olive oil and then attempt to either pin their opponents to the ground or lift them up and walk three steps. Most of that time is spent by the athletes trying to find just the right moment to make their move. Grease wrestling has been a part of Turkish culture since ancient times. The first game was hosted in 1362, so it is considered the world's oldest continual sporting event.

In the past, these slippery wrestling matches would last days. Today, there is a time limit of forty minutes. Held during the hottest months of the year, wrestlers are not allowed to stop for breaks or even a drink of water. The champion of the match gets prize money and is often sought after to be a coach or trainer for future wrestlers.

everything from rock to classical music festivals every summer. Antalya offers opera and ballet, while Izmir hosts the oldest festival active in the country, the Izmir International Fair in September, as well as the annual Izmir European Jazz Festival. Turkish pop music has also made its mark, with performers such as Tarkan and Kenan Dogulu producing smash hits in Europe.

Along with music comes dancing. Traditional folk music and dancing is often seen at weddings and at local festivals. At the same time, belly dancing and ballet are featured in city theaters, and Ankara even has its own ballet school.

Turkey's film industry got a slow start, with few films being made until the 1950s. After that, the industry took off, and Turkey quickly became one of the biggest film producers in the world. One of the most popular films in recent years is *Conquest 1453*, about the taking of Constantinople by Sultan Mehmed II. This movie is the highest-earning Turkish film in the country's history. *Conquest 1453* has been such a hit in Turkey that it has inspired a television show, and many Turks have organized clubs to reenact the battles in the film. Faruk Aksoy, the director of the movie, said, "The Turks are proud about the conquest because it not only changed our history but it also changed the world."

Turkey has also produced some critically acclaimed directors. Nuri Bilge Ceylan, who was a photographer before turning to film, is known for his poetic movies that focus on the details of people's lives. Ceylan has frequently been honored at the Cannes Film Festival, one of the world's leading

Bodrum Amphitheater

If you happen to be in the city of Bodrum, you can go to a concert in the very same amphitheater that was built way back in the fourth century BCE. Constructed during the reign of King Mausolus, this concert hall is one of the best-preserved buildings in all of Turkey. During the Roman period, the theater was enlarged to seat about thirteen thousand people. The site has been completely restored, and since 1973, it has been used as an open-air museum that hosts musical performances each year.

The amphitheater has three sections: the stage, the orchestra pit, and the seating for audiences. Some of the seats have names carved into them; perhaps they are the names of people who donated money centuries ago to help pay for the construction. That is a tradition that is still in practice today!

film festivals. In 2014, his film *Winter Sleep* won the Palme d'Or, the festival's top prize. The movie explores the life of a wealthy, self-absorbed hotel owner. Ceylan's other award-winning films include *Distant* and *Once Upon a Time in Anatolia*.

Arts and Crafts

A trip to the Grand Bazaar in Istanbul is a reminder that the Turks have a long tradition of producing many remarkable arts and crafts, such as complex woven rugs and ceramics. Ottoman buildings such as Topkapi Palace, where the sultan lived in Istanbul, include room after room decorated with

Many Turkish palaces, mosques, and tombs are covered in colorful, intricate tiles.

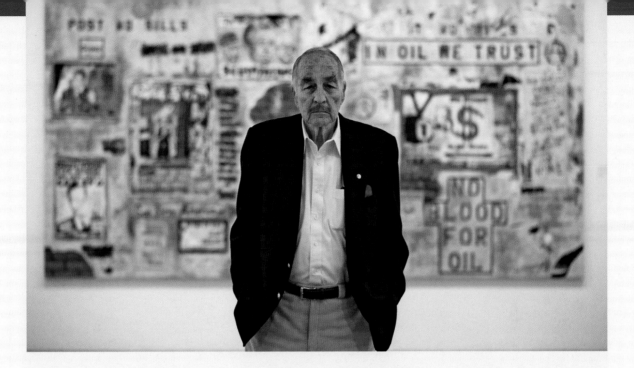

The Loss of a Legendary Artist

By the time he turned twenty-one years old, Burhan Dogancay had already played football for Ankara, earned a law degree from Ankara University, and moved to Paris, France. In his twenties, he earned a second degree, this time in economics, and began taking art classes. Art was what spoke to him the most, and by 1964, he had dedicated his life to it.

Born in 1929 in Istanbul, Dogancay lived and worked in both his homeland and the United States. When it came to painting, his canvas of choice was quite unusual. Dogancay was fascinated by large walls he came across in the middle of cities, and he used those for his art. The more colorful graffiti and torn posters there were on the walls, the better. Dogancay believed these walls were a reflection of culture and liked that his art would be exposed to nature's elements—and people's messages. "The walls I am drawn to have been worked on by nature and by human beings, so that they provide

a mirror of their respective neighborhoods," Dogancay once said. "They are speaking walls."

He continued, "Wall messages are constantly changing, new ones replacing old ones, old ones covered up or distorted by the elements. The whole human experience has been reflected on walls, beginning with cave drawings."

Dogancay traveled the world for years, taking photographs of walls in more than five hundred cities. He used these images to make more than four thousand collages and paintings.

In 1982, Dogancay exhibited his work in a show called *Walls That Whisper, Shout, and Sing*. In 2009, one of his paintings, *Blue Symphony*, was sold for $1.7 million in his hometown. His work has been displayed in more than seventy museums worldwide, and Istanbul has a museum dedicated to his works. He died in early 2013 as one of the country's most cherished artists.

An artisan decorates a copper tray. Creating copper goods is a traditional craft in Turkey.

fabulous ceramic tiles. Other traditional Turkish crafts include painted miniatures, engraved wood, metal jewelry, and stained glass. Islamic art tends to focus on geometric patterns, using vibrant colors. In Turkey, artists often turn paper into art by marbling the pages or adding ornate writing called calligraphy.

Some Turks make beautiful musical instruments using a combination of wood, animal horns and bones, and plants. Others weave baskets out of reeds and willows, carve complex gravestones, and use copper to make a variety of kitchen utensils.

On the Page
The earliest Turkish writings were poetry and oral stories that were eventually put onto paper. Fuzuli, a sixteenth-century poet, wrote in Arabic, Persian, and Turkish. During the Ottoman period, books about religion became popular.

Telling Tales

Two of the world's great storytellers—who may or may not have actually existed—may have been born in what is now Turkey. One was the blind poet Homer (below), who is believed to have been born between the twelfth and the eighth centuries BCE. Precisely where is a mystery, as seven different cities have claimed him, including the city of Izmir. Homer is said to have written the epic Greek poems *The Iliad* and *The Odyssey*, which tell of the adventures of Odysseus as he traveled around the world encountering everything from monsters to mermaids. The poems also detail the Trojan War.

The other famous storyteller was Aesop (above), who is believed to have been born around 600 BCE, perhaps in Thrace. Aesop is credited with writing more than one hundred Greek fables that teach lessons about life. Have you heard the story about the race between the tortoise and the hare, or the story of the unlikely friendship between the lion and the mouse? Those are Aesop's fables. The stories generally end with a moral, or life lesson, such as "Slow and steady wins the race" and "A kindness is never wasted."

In 1975, the history of the country's literature changed when Orhan Pamuk decided to become a writer instead of an architect and artist. In 1982, he published a novel, *Cevdet Bey and His Sons*, about a wealthy Istanbul family. It won awards, as did the novels that followed, and soon Pamuk was known internationally. His greatest novels, such as *My Name Is Red*, often touch on being lost between different cultures. In 2006, he won the Nobel Prize in Literature, the world's most prestigious award for writers, becoming the second-youngest person ever to receive the award.

Not all Turkish writing is serious. Aziz Nesin is an award-winning author of often humorous short stories and the founder of an organization dedicated to providing schooling and care for homeless children.

Many Turks enjoy the tales of Nasreddin Hodja, a trickster and wise man who was supposed to have lived during the thirteenth century. His adventures were turned into more than 350 stories. Here is an example of one:

> *The Hodja, bruised and limping, came upon a neighbor at the marketplace.*
>
> *"My dear friend, what happened to you?" asked the neighbor.*
>
> *The Hodja answered, "Last night my wife grew angry and kicked my robe down the stairs."*
>
> *"But how could that have caused your injuries?" continued the neighbor.*
>
> *"I was wearing the robe when she kicked it down the stairs," explained the Hodja.*

Comic Book Hero

You already know about Superman, Batman, Spiderman, and Iron Man. Now meet Tarkan, a Turkish comic book superhero drawn by Sezgin Burak. First created in the 1960s, Tarkan has become popular once again. The character is a warrior during the time of Attila the Hun. He is raised by wolves and grows up a loner, with only his wolf, Kurt, for a companion.

In his adventures, he battles hungry dragons and wicked sorcerers, along with a series of Romans and Vikings. Tarkan also takes care of a magical sword.

The Tarkan comic books became hugely popular, and several Tarkan movies were made between 1969 and 1973.

A new, younger Turkish hero has recently entered the comic world. HeroTurk and his friends from Greece, China, and Nigeria travel the world meeting famous historical figures and having adventures. "There was a lack of a Turkish hero appealing to children," says Fehmi Demirbag, one of the creators of HeroTurk. "HeroTurk is the first Turkish child hero."

CHAPTER 10

Turkish Ways

WHEREVER YOU TRAVEL IN THE WORLD, YOU will find that people celebrate important moments and take time to relax with family and friends. This is true in Turkey, where family gatherings are common, and men sometimes spend hours in coffee shops talking and playing cards.

In Turkey, people also take time to be kind to strangers. Knock on the door of almost any home in Turkey and you would most likely be heartily welcomed. Although much has changed in the country in the last century, some traditions, like this one, have stayed the same.

Home Sweet Home

In Turkey, the style of traditional homes varies greatly from one region to the next. For centuries, Turks built homes from whatever materials they found in their area, whether it was

Opposite: **A tram travels down a busy street in Istanbul.**

stone, wood, mud, or brick. In rural Anatolia, one-third of the village homes were made out of adobe mud-brick, a material made of mud, pieces of straw, and dried plants. Roofs were flat and made out of branches or plants and then covered with clay. This allowed families to sleep on the roof on hot nights, or use the space to dry food.

In the Taurus Mountains, the Aegean, and parts of eastern Anatolia, stone is plentiful, so it was used to make houses. In the Black Sea region, houses tend to be made of wood held together with clamps or nails. Gaps between the wood slats

All of the old buildings in Mardin, in southeastern Anatolia, are built from limestone rock quarried in the area.

Beehive Houses

In southeastern Anatolia, in the city of Harran, close to the Syrian border, ancient and very practical houses still stand. These are beehive homes, cone-shaped houses made of little more than mud and water, baked hard by the constant sunshine. These homes date back as far as 300 BCE. The homes needed to be able to withstand the strong winds and the rumbling of possible earthquakes. Wood was scarce in the area, so people depended on shaping homes from the material they had—adobe brick mud.

The houses are extremely practical for the region. The homes have few windows and small doors to keep out the day's heat and glare. The roofs are sloped so that when it rains, the torrential waters rush off before they can loosen the mud. Above all, this type of home is fast and easy to build.

Although the houses look simple from the outside, they are quite elaborate on the inside. They contain hearths, or fireplaces, used for cooking and heating, as well as platforms for sleeping, and pits in the floor for storing grain. Many of these beehive homes are split-level style, with bedrooms upstairs. No one lives in the homes today. They are open for tourists to walk through and appreciate a distant way of life.

Colorful apartment buildings rise on the outskirts of Istanbul.

are typically filled with small stones, mud plaster, or dried plants. In the hottest parts of the country, the gaps are sometimes left open to allow for better airflow. The homes closest to the coastlines are occasionally built on stilts to protect the buildings from flooding.

In the big cities, most homes are made of bricks. A growing number of people live in high-rise apartment buildings.

An Unexpected Fee

Public bathrooms in Turkey are not free like they are in the United States. The bathrooms found in subways, malls, shopping centers, and bus terminals, for example, require a fee of 35 to 50 cents to use. Toilet paper sometimes requires an extra fee. The restrooms generally have attendants to whom you hand your coins on the way in or out.

Family Life

When a woman gets pregnant in Turkey, she often announces it to the world with pride by wearing either a special bracelet from her mother-in-law or another symbol, such as a special scarf. Once the baby is born, more gifts follow for mother and child. Some families also plant trees in honor of the new child. The baby's name is usually selected by an elder in the family, while words from the Qur'an are whispered into his or her ear.

Some families in smaller towns and villages still follow the tradition of choosing a husband or wife for their children. Even when the young people choose their own partners, it is common for the families to get together to formally ask permission.

Family is important in Turkey, and grandmothers often look after their grandchildren.

In Turkey, the elderly usually move in with their children to help with household chores and take care of grandchildren. Nursing homes are considered shameful in the smaller villages, although they are becoming much more common in the larger cities.

In Turkey, most funerals follow Muslim practice. Before being buried, the person's body is washed and then wrapped in sheets. Next, the body is placed in a coffin and brought to a mosque. After prayers, the casket is carried to the graveyard. Many Muslims do not want to be buried in a casket, preferring instead to be in the soil, covered with stones. They believe this is closer to God.

Men carry a coffin out of a mosque following a funeral. They will then take the coffin to a cemetery for burial.

The Hamam

In Turkey, the public bath, or *hamam*, was once an important part of the country's culture. People participated for a number of reasons. It was a social activity, a chance to visit with friends. It was done to improve health by relaxing muscles and increasing blood flow. Finally, it was done for spiritual reasons, to enhance cleanliness and purity.

What was it like to have a traditional Turkish bath? You can find out for yourself. Traditional public baths still exist in Turkey, but they are used mainly by tourists. First, you undress and put on slippers and a cotton wrap called a *pestemal*. Attendants provide soap, shampoo, and a towel.

After changing, your first stop is a warm, humid room designed to help you relax. You are instructed to lie down on a heated platform. It's time to sweat! Next, your attendant guides you to a basin and scrubs you head to foot with a handwoven washcloth called a *kese*. Using a thin cloth full of soap, the attendant blows and creates thousands of bubbles that cover every inch of you.

After being rinsed with warm water, it is time for a massage. And then, finally, it is time to cool down. After being led to a cool room, you are given some cool juice or tea to drink. You have reached the end of your traditional Turkish experience!

Many Turkish meals begin with meze, an array of small dishes. These might include spreads, salads, cheeses, and small meatballs.

On the Table

When you think of Turkish food, you might think about the intense sweetness of Turkish delight, the dark richness of Turkish coffee, or the grilled meat and vegetables of *shish kebabs*. In Turkey, it is easy to find these and many other delicious foods.

Kebabs are different from one region to another in Turkey. The dish is always meat, usually stewed or grilled, and most commonly lamb. It is sometimes combined with tomatoes, onions, or peppers. The dark purple eggplant is a favorite throughout the country, and is often used in salads or is turned into a spread for bread. *Cacik* is also a common dish. This refreshing yogurt and mint dish can be eaten on its own, used as a dip, or mixed with other foods. Bread is served with most meals.

Other favorites in Turkey include *dolma*, a dish made of vegetables and rice and wrapped up in grape or cabbage leaves, and *borek*, a combination of thin, flaky layers of dough with cheese, spinach, spices, and ground meat. People along the Black Sea eat a wide variety of seafood, including anchovies, octopus, mussels, and squid.

The southwestern area is known for its *lahmacun*, which is like pizza, and the east is known for spicy dishes. Turks often drink coffee, tea, and fruit juices. Large cities have a number of snack stands selling tasty treats such as fresh almonds or *simit*, a sesame-covered bread ring. Over the years, a growing number of fast-food restaurants have opened in Turkey.

A street vendor sells simit from a cart. Simit has been made in Istanbul since the 1500s.

Time to Eat!

Cacik is a delicious yogurt dish. Eat it on its own as an appetizer, or serve it on the side with kebabs, rice, eggplant, or practically any other dish. Have an adult help you with this recipe.

Ingredients

2 cups plain yogurt

2 tablespoons olive oil

2 cloves garlic, diced

3 cucumbers, peeled and diced

1 tablespoon fresh mint, finely chopped

½ teaspoon salt

Directions

Put the yogurt, oil, and garlic in a large bowl and mix until smooth. Add the cucumbers, mint, and salt and mix thoroughly. Chill in the refrigerator for at least an hour before serving. Enjoy!

Holidays in Turkey

New Year's Day	January 1
National Sovereignty and Children's Day	April 23
Ataturk, Youth, and Sports Day	May 19
Victory Day	August 30
Republic Day	October 29

Just like other countries, Turkey has special dishes that are associated with certain holidays. At the end of Ramadan, many families prepare a dessert called *ashure*. This pudding includes a mix of many ingredients, including peas, beans, almonds, rice, raisins, rose water, pomegranate seeds, orange peels, and cinnamon. Almost all weddings include a special soup made of lamb, lemon juice, eggs, flour, butter, and red pepper.

Let's Play!

The children in Turkey enjoy playing many of the same games that children play elsewhere. Games like hide-and-seek, leapfrog, ring around the rosie (above), and blind man's bluff are common, although they have different names.

In Turkey, a game similar to London Bridge is known as *ac kapiyi bezirgan basi* or "open the door, head merchant." At least eight children are needed to play this game. Two children are selected and choose names for themselves. One is usually "golden watch" and the other "golden bracelet." These two children hold their hands together like a bridge, and others file under one by one, saying, "Open the door, head merchant!" The kids holding hands reply, "I'll open it, but what will you give me?" The other children then reply, "Take the scoundrel behind me!" Everyone says, "One rat, two rats, three rats," and whichever child is under the bridge at the end of the rhyme is caught. The children making the bridge then ask whether the child who has been caught prefers a golden watch or golden bracelet. The child stands in a line behind whichever player represents the item he or she chooses. The game continues until all the players have been caught and are in line.

Then comes the second part of the game. A stick or other marker is put on the ground between the two lines. The children in each line grasp each other by the waist while the two leaders grab each others' hands. The two lines then pull in opposite directions like in tug-of-war. Whichever team pulls the leader over the marker on the ground wins!

A Mix of Styles

No one style of dress dominates in Turkey. In cities, people tend to dress casually but stylishly. Some observant Muslim women wear a head scarf with their modern clothes. The scarf covers only their hair. Others also cover their clothes with a long, straight coat called a *jilbab*. Still other women wear a *chador*, a long, loose robe that covers their hair and body.

The farther east one is in Turkey, the more likely women are to cover more of their body in a loose-fitting way. But even in Istanbul, styles change from one neighborhood to the next, and some parts of the city are a teeming mix. Turkey truly is a crossroads: a complex and intriguing blend of traditional and modern, East and West, Europe and Asia.

Traditional and modern meet on the streets of Istanbul.

Fast Facts

Official name: Republic of Turkey

Capital: Ankara

Official language: Turkish, Kurdish

Ankara

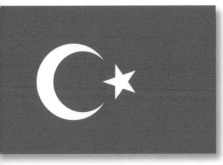

National flag

Mediterranean coast

Official religion:	None
Year of founding:	1923
National anthem:	"Istiklal Marsi" ("Independence March")
Type of government:	Parliamentary democracy
Head of state:	President
Head of government:	Prime minister
Area of country:	302,535 square miles (783,562 sq km)
Latitude and longitude of geographic center:	39° N, 35° E
Bordering countries:	Greece to the west; Bulgaria to the northwest; Georgia to the northeast; Armenia, Azerbaijan, and Iran to the east; and Iraq and Syria to the southeast
Highest elevation:	Mount Ararat 16,949 feet (5,166 m)
Lowest elevation:	Sea level, along the coasts
Average high temperature:	In Ankara, 40°F (4°C) in January, 86°F (30°C) in July; in Izmir, 55°F (13°C) in January, 92°F (33°C) in July
Average low temperature:	In Ankara, 27°F (–3°C) in January, 61°F (16°C) in July; in Izmir, 43°F (6°C) in January, 73°F (23°C) in July
Average annual rainfall:	Along coastal areas, rainfall can reach 113 inches (287 cm) a year; the national average is 14.7 inches (37.3 cm)

Cappadocia

Currency

National population (2013 est.):	76.7 million	
Population of major cities (2012 est.):	Istanbul	13,710,512
	Ankara	4,630,735
	Izmir	3,401,994
	Bursa	1,983,880
	Adana	1,636,220

Landmarks:
- ▶ *Blue Mosque*, Istanbul
- ▶ *Cappadocia*, Nevsehir
- ▶ *Ephesus*, Selcuk
- ▶ *Grand Bazaar*, Istanbul
- ▶ *Topkapi Palace*, Istanbul
- ▶ *Troy*, near Canakkale

Economy: Services account for about 64 percent of the country's economy, industry makes up 27 percent, and agriculture just over 9 percent. Tourism, finance, and trade are important in Turkey. Major manufacturing industries include textiles, foods and beverages, motor vehicles, and steel. Important crops include sugar beets, wheat, barley, tomatoes, olives, hazelnuts, and apricots. Sheep, cattle, and dairy products are also important.

Currency: The Turkish lira. In 2014, 1 Turkish lira equaled 45 cents, and 1 U.S. dollar equaled 2.24 lira.

System of weights and measures: Metric system

Literacy rate: 94%

Schoolchildren

Orhan Pamuk

Common Turkish words and phrases:

Merhaba	Hello
Elveda	Good-bye
Hos geldiniz	Welcome
Hos bulduk	Happy to be here.
Nasilsin?	How are you?
Iyiyim	I am fine
Tesekkur ederim	Thank you

Prominent Turks:

Mustafa Kemal Ataturk (1881–1938)
Founder of modern Turkey

Mevlana Celaleddin-i Rumi (1207–1273)
Sufi poet

Recep Tayyip Erdogan (1954–)
Prime minister

Orhan Pamuk (1952–)
Nobel Prize–winning novelist

Cagan Sekercioglu (1975–)
Ornithologist and wildlife researcher

Mimar Sinan (1489–1588)
Architect

Naim Suleymanoglu (1967–)
Weight lifter

To Find Out More

Books

▶ Ali-Karamali, Sumbul. *Growing Up Muslim: Understanding the Beliefs and Practices of Islam*. New York: Delacourt Press, 2012.

▶ Shields, Sarah. *Turkey*. Washington, DC: National Geographic Children's Books, 2009.

▶ Thompson, Jan. *Islam*. Toronto, Canada: Whitecap Books, 2010.

▶ Ural, Serpil. *Folktales of Turkey: From Agri and Zelve*. Istanbul: Citlembik Publications, 2012.

Music

▶ Du-Sems Ensemble. *Traditional Turkish Sufi Music*. West Sussex, UK: ARC Music, 2012.

▶ *The Rough Guide to the Music of Turkey*. London: World Music Network, 2003.

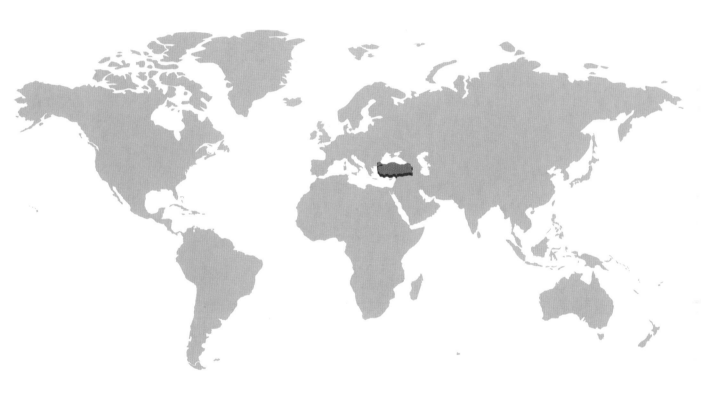

▶ Visit this Scholastic Web site for more information on Turkey:
www.factsfornow.scholastic.com
Enter the keyword **Turkey**

Index

Page numbers in *italics*
indicate illustrations.

national, 125, *125*
religious, 91
Homer, 111, *111*
housing, 24, 25, 80, 115–116, *116*, 117, *117*, 118, *118*
hydroelectricity, 25, 26
hyenas, 25

I

Iliad, The (Homer), 111
Ilisu Dam, 25
Ilkkaracan, Ipek, 74
insect life, 30
Internet, 57, *57*
Internet Technologies Association, 57
Iron Age, 40
Islamic religion. *See also* religion.
  Abu Bakr, 95
  Adnan Menderes and, *52*
  Alevism, 95
  Antatolia region and, 100
  calendar, 91
  charity and, 93
  clothing and, 56–57, 66, *66*, 127, *127*
  Five Pillars of Islam, 91–93
  funerals, 120, *120*
  government and, 53, 54, 55–57, 59
  Grand Mosque, 22
  Great Mosque and Hospital of Divrigi, 98, *98*
  holidays, 91
  imams (religious leaders), *94*
  membership of, 89
  military coups and, 53, 54
  minarets (mosque towers), 88
  mosques, 9, 22, 45, *45*, 47, 67, 88, *91, 92, 92, 94, 98, 98, 120*
  Muhammad (prophet), 90, 91–92, 94–95
  national flag and, 64
  pilgrimage to Mecca, 93
  prayer, 92–93, *92*

Qur'an (holy book), 90, 91, 92, 119
Ramadan, 93, *93*
Seljuq Empire and, 45, 100
Shi'ism, 95, *95*
Sufism, 96–98, *96*
Sunnism, 95
Treaty of Lausanne and, 51
women and, 56–57, 66, *66*, 127, *127*
Istanbul. *See also* cities.
  Allied occupation of, 49–50
  architecture in, 108
  Armenian Apostolic Church, 100, *101*
  Basilica Cistern, 44, *44*
  Beyoglu neighborhood, *15*
  Blue Mosque, 22, *22*
  as Byzantium, 22, 43
  children in, *102*
  Church of the Holy Wisdom, 22, 45, *45*
  clothing in, 127
  as Constantinople, 11, 22, 43–44, 45, 46, 99, 100, 107
  elections in, 64
  Global Summit of Women, 74
  Grand Bazaar, 8, 9–15, *12*, 22, 108
  housing, *118*
  Istanbul Museum of Modern Art, 18
  Istanbul Technical University, 74
  Istanbul Tulip Festival, 31
  Istanbul University, 83
  location of, 9, 20
  Mehmed the Conqueror and, 10, *11*
  military coup and, 53
  mosques, 9, 22, *22*, 45, *45, 92, 94*
  music in, 105–106
  Ottoman Empire and, 10, *11*, 22, 46

population of, 22, 44, 80
Ramadan in, 93
roadways, *102*
Sakirin Mosque, 92
soccer teams in, 104
Spice Market, 22
Topkapi Palace, 108
trams, *114*
"Istiklal Marsi" (national anthem), 62
Italy, 75, 49
Izmir, 22, 80, 106, 111
Izmir European Jazz Festival, 106
Izmir International Fair, 106
Izmit, 27

J

jereed (sport), 104–105
jilbab (clothing), 127
Judaism, 98
judicial branch of government, 60, 65, *65*
Justinian I (Byzantine emperor), 44, *44*

K

Kapalicarsi. See Grand Bazaar.
Kars Province, 33
Kars region, 33–34
Karst, 21
kebabs (food), 122
Kemal, Mustafa. *See* Ataturk.
Kizil River, 19
Kocatepe Mosque, 67
Konya, 23
Kurdish people, 54, 55, 56, 57, 80, 81, *81*

L

lahmacun (food), 123
Lake Kuyucuk, 33, *33*
Lake Van, 19, 24
languages, 12, 41, 45, 62, 81, 83, 84–87, *84, 85*
legislative branch of government, 52, 60

literacy rate, 82, 86
literature, 110, 111, *111*, 112–113, *112*, 133, *133*
Little Ararat peak, 24
livestock, *26*, 71, 81
lodos (winds), 27
loggerhead turtles, 35–37, *36*

M
magnesite, 72
Mamak Landfill, 75
manufacturing, 22, 69, 71, 72, 74, 75
maps. *See also* historical maps.
    Ankara, *67*
    geopolitical, *10*
    population density, *80*
    resources, *72*
    topographical, *19*
Mardin, *78*, *116*
marine life, 29, 30, 35–37, *35*, 41
Marmara region, 18, 20, 26
Marmara University, 83
Marmaray Project, 73, *73*
marriages, 119, 125
Mausoleum of Halicarnassus, 42, *42*
Mausolus (Persian governor), 42
Mediterranean region, 20–21, 26–27, 40
Mediterranean Sea, *16*, 17, 20, *36*, 37, 46
Mehmed the Conqueror, 10, *11*
Mehmed II (sultan), 107
Melek, Melike Turhan, 98
Menderes, Adnan, *52*, 53
methane, 75
meze (foods), *122*
Middle East Technical University, 83
Miletus, 40
military, 48, 53, *53*, 54, *54*, 61
mining, 71, 72
Mongols, 46, *46*
monk seals, 37, *37*
mosaics, 45
mosques, 9, 22, *22*, 45, *45*, 47, 67, 88, 91, 92, *92*, 94, 98, *98*, *120*
mountain gazelles, 35

Mount Ararat, 19, 24, *24*
Muhammad (prophet), 90, 91–92, 94–95
Museum of Anatolian Civilizations, 67, *67*
museums, 18, 101, *101*, 107, *107*
music, 62, 105–106
My Name Is Red (Orhan Pamuk), 112

N
names, 82, 119
national anthem, 62
national flag, 62, 64, *64*
national flower, 31, *31*, 71
National Geographic magazine, 29
national holidays, 125, *125*
nationalism, *49*, 50
Nesin, Aziz, 112–113
Nicholas (saint), 100, *100*
Noah's Ark, 24
Nobel Prize, 112
nomads, 81

O
Odyssey, The (Homer), 111
oil industry, 55
olives, 18, 41
Olympic Games, 103
Once Upon a Time in Anatolia (film), 108
Order of Mevlana, 97
Orhan I (Mongol prince), 46
Orthodox Church, 43
Osman (Mongol prince), 46
Ottoman Empire
    Abdulhamid II, 48
    architecture, 47
    Constantinople and, *11*
    constitution of, 48
    economy of, 47–48
    Grand Bazaar and, 10
    Istanbul and, 10, *11*, 22, 46
    jereed (sport), 104–105
    map, 48
    Mehmed the Conqueror, 10, *11*

national flag and, 64
nationalist movement and, 50
Suleyman the Magnificent, 46–47, *47*
Sumela Monastery and, 101, *101*
World War I and, 48–49

P
Pamukkale hot springs, 76
Pamuk, Orhan, 112, *112*, 133, *133*
parrot fish, *35*
people. *See also* women.
    Arabs, 81
    Armenians, 45, 46, 49, 81
    children, 61, 74, 79, 82, 83, 87, *102*, 119, *119*, 126, *126*
    clothing, 56, 127, *127*
    cost of living, 77
    education, 61, 81, 82–83, *82*, *83*, 87
    elderly, 79, 86, *86*, 120
    families, 61, 115, 119, *119*
    foods, 93, *93*, 122–123, *122*, 124, *124*
    funerals, 120, *120*
    Greeks, 40–41, 45, 49–50, *50*, 51, 81, 101
    health care, 98, *98*
    housing, 24, 25, 80, 115–116, *116*, 117, *117*, 118, *118*
    jobs, 11, 74, *74*, 75, 80
    kindness of, 115
    Kurds, 54, 55, 56, 57, 80, 81, *81*
    languages, 12, 41, 45, 62, 81, 83, 84–87, *84*, *85*
    literacy rate, 82, 86
    marriages, 119, 125
    Mongols, 46, 46
    names, 82, 119
    nomads, 81
    population, 22, 24, 44, 67, 79–80, *80*

Meet the Author

TAMRA ORR IS A FULL-TIME AUTHOR living in the Pacific Northwest. Orr graduated from Ball State University and moved from Indiana to Oregon in 2001. She is the author of more than 350 educational books for readers of all ages. She loves learning more about the world around her. While researching this book, she especially enjoyed the chance to sip sweet Turkish coffee while nibbling on a piece of Turkish delight. It's a perfect combination! It was a pleasure to return to reading about Turkey after writing about it for Children's Press in 2003. Since then, she has written about more than a dozen other countries and continues to be amazed at how diverse and beautiful the world can be.

Photo Credits